# Spiritual Warfare

(With excerpts from The Battle For Life, and The Mystery of Christ In You.)

ISBN 13:    978-0-9970856-2-4
ISBN 10:    0997085622

Printed in the United States of America
Published by Ecclesia Publishing House LLC

# Table of Contents

# Chapter One

## Spiritual Freedom

"The pride of your heart has  deceived you…"---Obad. 1.3.

Let us not leave any stone unturned to get to the source of so much wretchedness. Why is it that most of us Christians have no power over sin in our lives? We are not only talking about the leadership falling into disgrace, but the rest of us---maybe not on the evening news---but nevertheless falling short of the glory and expectations of God. We need more power for our Christian Life. One of the weapons in Satan's arsenal of evil is spiritual pride. Pride is not only one of his weapons, it was the main reason he was thrown out of Heaven.

Therefore, pride is a part of his personality; it is very powerful when working in the self-life of human beings. It makes no difference whether the human being is a Christian or not, spiritual pride operates through the Law of Sin and Death, and is a personality defect that has to be dealt with in our Christian Life.

What exactly is deception? Obviously it is the process or state of being deceived. The Webster Dictionary describes it as, "To believe what is false or invalid; to be misled; or to be ensnared; to deliberately misrepresent facts by works or actions in order to further one's own interest; other, beguile, mislead, delude."

The biblical example of this phenomenon is recorded in Gen. 3.13, where Eve confessed, "The serpent beguiled {(deceived, tricked} me, and I did eat." She was the first human being to be deceived; though in Heaven, the serpent, being Satan, introduced deception to the angelic realm, and was cast out of Heaven because of it: "Satan which deceives the whole world (Rev. 12.9).

Cain was too proud to take even God's advice and rethink his present course of action, and line up with the acceptable Word of God. God told him that a deceiver, the spirit of pride was crouched like a tiger outside his door; it was waiting to devour him; but God counseled Cain not to give in to the evil spirit, but resist it by Faith and confidence in the revealed Word of God.

However, Cain did not take God seriously, but went out and killed Abel. He ruined his Calling and Commission, his opportunity at ministering to humanity.

There are many ways that a spirit of pride can enter us, but it is first introduced through some type of deception, a single or set of lies, values, postulates, theories, philosophies or beliefs, that we have reckoned as unquestionable truth, and are making important decisions based on them; which means that we gave the spirit of deception control of us and our ministry decisions through this "hook" that this spirit has in our heart.

For example, we may not believe that women can be effective ministers based on what we think of women who have hurt us, or a mother that was, controlling, emotional or mentally unstable. It's not that we hate women, but we don't believe that they are emotionally equipped to handle the demands of pasturing a church and counseling hurting people; and so we come up with this "reasonable" explanation that seems "biblical" when in fact it is demonic!

The spirit of deception can also opens the door to rebellion, which lets in a spirit of pride, and pride will cause us to be insanely affixed on ourselves, our physical appearance, finances, family successes, linage, vocations, degrees, social and political connections, material property, vehicles, our "stadium-size "ministry, and our "perceived" popularity.

We become more interested in acquiring loyal "fans" than saving souls and mentoring young ministers. Sometimes we are patted on the back by our fans so much that we walk slightly bent over! Yet we are spiritual criminals. We strut around with our armed body guards when the real enemy is within us; we are the one most hazardous to our health; we are the one toxic to those around us; and we are the one who need to be delivered.

We preach and people throw money at our feet; we are on television as a Christian celebrity. We believe our own hype and publicity. We have forgotten where we came from, as sinners, and Who it was who loved and saved us. We are more concerned with selling books, CDs and other merchandise than the sick, seniors, addicts and others in need.

Many of us are terrified to use our fortune and connections to help a struggling minister or ministry, for fear that minister will one day become as prosperous as us, an equal, or yet, a better minister that us; so we don't help them in order to keep them looking up to us; we make them promises with no intentions of keeping them: "They must remain a fan."

In Num. 32.23 warns us that "...your sins shall find you out. Whatever spirit drives us will one day expose us for the person that we really are, that is, the person we have become. It's the duty and nature of evil spirits to deceive and then expose us; as a toaster toasts bread because it was manufactured for that purpose, so is the evil spirit of pride bent on exposing us.

The Word in Pro. 16.18 confirms this: "Pride goes before destruction, and a haughty spirit before a fall. And 1 Cor. 10.12 reads: "Wherefore let him who thinks he stands take heed lest he fall." Spiritual pride paralyzes the leadership, and then we the congregation are little more than worshippers of the leader and not true worshippers of Christ---making flesh our arm to lean on.

If we think that we are all that and a bag of potato chips we are mistaken. If we persist in this type of behavior, the Word says "take heed" because we are about to fall---and hard! Few ministers fully recover their status and ministry after a national scandal. God may still use us, but not nearly as much as before. For example, we may go from preaching to 300 million souls worldwide, down to preaching to fifty souls in a small church.

The spirit of pride releases a strange power and counterfeit anointing in the congregation, and we find ourselves deceived into believing that it is the Presence of the Holy Spirit. Even counterfeit prophetic utterances come forth in such a pseudo environment; we become more enslaved, bound to that ministry---not because God told us to stay there---but because of witchcraft!

Spiritual pride opens the door for other spirits to enter the leader and the congregation; these spirits include religious spirits, lying, greed, jealousy perversion, sickness, disease and other hateful demons. As deceived leaders we proclaim that "Everything you need is in the house!" We said it to imply that we have all the Spiritual Gifts, spiritual knowledge, wisdom, mantles, divine revelation and counsel. This is a lie. We said it to keep our people from experiencing the fullness of Jesus' manifestations in other ministries; we said it because of insecurity; we want our membership not to give money, time and presence elsewhere; also, as leaders we already know that other ministers in the area have Spiritual Gifts, mantles, teaching and preaching skills that we are envious of, and so we discourages our members from experiencing the power of Christ that blankets the entire Body.

### Pride in a Christian

The following are examples of Spiritual Pride: Deceived to think we are self-sufficient; Feel that we don't need the Church; Want to be a leader but doesn't need the training; Will not receive instruction, correction and is unteachable; The leaders are always wrong and we are always right; We are perfect as we are; We rebel against civil and Christian authority; Have an inflated opinion of self; thinks everyone else is less spiritual, less intelligent, inferior or ignorant; Can't face the biblical truth about ourselves; Think we know the Bible better than everyone;

Blames others for our failures; Won't take personal responsibility; Is selfish and self-glorious, or think we are "fabulous;" Claim to "daily" receive "personal" visitations from Jesus, extraordinary visions or being taught personally by Jesus (as Paul was); Seldom repents even when caught doing wrong; justifies or minimizes; Claims to discover better or additional ways to hear from God, like the Koran, Masons, Horoscope, meditation and eastern philosophies;

Lacks self-discipline, control, an indulger in vices, but claim we are strong and these vices don't affect us like other Christians; Claim that we are the only one in our church that is Saved; Claim that all we need is Jesus and the King James Version Bible; Claim that we don't need to fast, pray, counseling, Inner Healing & Deliverance, because we are at some high level of Faith; Claim that we never sin; Claim to been granted an extraordinary title like: Exalted Bishop Chief-Apostle, and similar lofty titles (Jesus Christ is the only Chief Apostle).

## Combating Pride

"God resist the proud, but gives grace unto the humble. 7 Submit your selves therefore to God. Resist the devil, and he will flee from you. 8 Draw near to God, and He will draw near to you"--- Jam. 34.6,7,8.

Humility is the key to getting set free from the spirit of pride. If Cain would have humbled himself and listened to God, he would not have stepped out the door and been overwhelmed by the crouched tiger of pride. Humility of self allows the Grace--- unmerited favor---and power of God to cleanse the consciousness by the washing and regeneration of the Word. The Word will cleanse the mind from the demonically imposed sin-consciousness which is under the Law of Sin and Death, that is, a consciousness riddled with condemnation, guilt, shame, regret and other negative emotions---to a righteousness consciousness which is under the Law of the Spirit of Life.

Humility involves our submission to God, our activation of Faith in God and His Word to resist the Devil and his spirit of pride; he will have no legal right or hook in us, and will have to, by the Law of the Spirit of Life, leave us alone. As we draw near to God he draws near to us too; this decreases the ministry time tremendously, by bridging the gap-time between our distorted mind, and His Christ-Mind, Inner Healing and Deliverance power.

Fasting, prayer and reading the Word is the best way to draw near to God. We must sanctify ourselves, separate ourselves from the corrupting connections to the world---those connections that feed the prideful spirit; even a separation from the influences of other vain and conceited people whom we hang out with or associate with after work, in a lodge, frat or sorority house.

Repentance of pride and a sincere desire to change our lifestyle under the guidance of the Holy Spirit will start the cleansing process. a part of the local church is scriptural. Being under authority, possibly re-turning and apologizing to the church leader that God placed us under is also a good start. For the Word says to, "obey them that have the rule over you…" (Heb. 13.17). Fellowship and faithful service to the ministry will break the back of the spirit of pride and remove self-centered selfishness; as to "not forsaking the assembly of ourselves together… "---Heb.10.25.

The seeking and obtaining of Inner Healing and Deliverance can be described as this: "Let us draw near with a true heart in full assurance of faith, having our hearts sprinkled from an evil conscious, and our bodies washed with pure water" (Heb. 10.22. Inner Healing and Deliverance is the children's bread!

"Thy Word have I hid in mine heart, that I might not sin against Thee"---Ps. 119.11.

It does not go without mentioning, that we as Christians have a certain amount of "mental ascent" when it comes to the Word of God. We read and understand what the Bible teaches, but do not put that understanding into practice; whereas, the Word of God must be more than a philosophical idea but action; from action to practice, and from practice to a lifestyle. The deception and pride can be eliminated through Repentance, Faith and Prayer. But all these must be rooted in the Word of God, to have any lasting effect, because the Holy Spirit only operates by and through the Word of God.

If we wanted to be set free from whatever it is that binds us, what keeps us from living successfully in the Word, the Word of God must be taken seriously. Then we will be successful, prosperous and capable of fulfilling our destiny, the Calling and Commissioning that is on our life.

To begin with, we must be specific and stand on God's Word as the foundation of our thoughts, emotions, will, and imaginations (creativity); and pray according to the Word of God. The best way to pray according to the Word of God is to study the New Covenant, the Word of God as written in the New Testament. To conquer indwelling demon spirits that have latched onto us like swamp leeches, we must specifically follow the Word of God. In Mt. 4.4, Jesus states, "It is written, Man shall not live by bread alone, but by every word that proceeds out of the mouth of God." Jesus made this statement in response to an attack on His mind, will, emotion and empty, fasted stomach.

Satan tempted Jesus to use His authority solely to validate Himself, to satisfy his stomach, and to learn more about the "mystery" of the "Seed" that had been hidden from him for ages (Col. 1.26) prompted the curiosity of Satan. Initially, he wasn't 100% certain that Jesus is the Son.

Whereas, Jesus told Him that He was the Son of God because He refused to do what Satan told him! He was the only Man who could resist Satan. Jesus told him that all He was required to do was the will of His Father who sent Him. He wouldn't perform miracles solely for the sake of proving who He is, never before the one He came to destroy the works of.

"Then the devil takes Him up into the holy city, and sets Him on the pinnacle of the temple, and says to Him, If you are the Son of God, cast yourself down; for it is written, He shall give His angels charge concerning thee…" (Mt. 4.6,7). This took place after Jesus refused to turn the stones into food. Now, Satan tempted Jesus to put God to a foolish test concerning the Father's love, ability or willingness to protect His Son from danger or death.

"Again, the devil takes Him up into an exceeding high mountain, and shows Him all the kingdoms of the world, and the glory of them. And says unto Him, All these things will I give thee, if thou will fall down and worship me" (V. 8-11).

Jesus' response was most fittingly an example for us. He told the devil to get lost! More King James-like, "get thee hence." The devil took Jesus up on the mountain to show Him the "glory" the pride of owning the whole world, everything and everyone in it. It was pride that Satan wielded before Jesus, the same pride that got him thrown out of Heaven. He boasted of how it was handed to him (by Adam) and that he was in control of it; and all Jesus had to do to get it---NOW---was to bow down and worship him; Jesus didn't dispute his claim.

Many times, as Christians, Satan takes us up and sits us on a high pedestal and promises to give us what our flesh craves---popularity, money, power or sex---if we would bow down and worship him. He is able, via his territorial spirits, to deliver what he promises; but God is also able to deliver the promised judgment upon those of us who live for the devil and die in him---that judgment is Hell.

But the answer to this dilemma lies in Jesus' response: "Thou shall worship the Lord thy God, and Him only shall thou serve" (v.10). The goal of Satan is to get us to worship him; when we fall into sin and stay there, we are worshipping him. The occasional fall is not worship, but the habitual revisiting becomes a habit, then a lifestyle. The next thing we know we are far away from the narrow road.

And so, as Jesus utilized the Word of God to combat the advances of Satan, we can also use the Word of God to protect, deliver and rescue us from his temptations and traps. When we speak and pray the Word of God, tremendous power is released in our lives, power to destroy yokes and lift burdens.

Because the Word of God is a two-edged sword and our tongue is the member that wields it, we have to be careful that we are not just speaking the Word but doers of it too. If not, the same sword that loops of the heads of demons (figuratively) will loop our head off too! Inasmuch, as we are subject to obey the Word as demons are. Jesus was (and still is) a Man of Prayer; His life was one of fasting, prayer and fellowship with the Father.

He knows the worth of prayer---that it is priceless—and passes this truth on to us. Many times He had to get away from the crowds to spend time with the Father; the people, hungry for the Word, pressed in so that He had little time to eat, pray or even sleep.

Every great manifestation of God's Glory in the Old and New Testament was in response to fervent prayer. Abraham, Moses, David, Solomon, the Prophets and Apostles prayed the glory of God down, and changed their circumstances. After David committed adultery and murdered Uriah, Bathsheba's husband, he prayed this prayer of godly sorrow and repentance:

1 "Have mercy upon me, O God, according to thy loving kindness; according unto the multitude of thy tender mercies blot out my transgressions. 2 Wash me thoroughly from mine iniquity, and cleanse me from my sin. 3 For I acknowledge my transgressions; and my sin is ever before me. 7 Purge me 23with hyssop, and I shall be clean; wash me, and I shall be whiter than snow"---Ps. 51.1-3,7.

David is a good example of a man who did some lowdown, scandalous things, but when his head cleared, he realized what he had done and repented. Yet, according to God, David was a man after His own heart! David was human; so are we. And all that God requires when we sin is Repentance and Faith; both of these can be accomplished through humble prayer.

One reason why it is so hard for many of us to pray like David is because we are more sorry that we got caught then we are of the sin. We are reeling from the blow and effects of private or public disgrace than from godly sorrow. Still many of us find it hard to pray because of the spirit of pride saying, "You are pathetic!" And so the spirit of pride won't allow us to pour out our heart to the Lord and ask for forgiveness and cleansing which is also Inner Healing and Deliverance.

This is where the good fight of Faith comes in! If we really want to be delivered, we don't care with the demons say or what the people around us think. People don't know what we are going through; they don't know how good God has been to us; they weren't there when He saved our soul; and they weren't there when the rent, light bill, gas bill, phone bill and the car note was due; not to mention they weren't there when the cupboard was bare and our wallet was empty: But God showed up and He delivered us from the trials, tribulations, situations,  snares, addictions and from criminals!

Saints, God knows what we need to get back on track. In Jn. 16.23, He says to "Ask, Seek and Knock." Having Faith in God we ask for cleansing, Inner Healing and Deliverance; we seek first the Kingdom and its righteousness believing that all the other things we need will be added accordingly. We speak words impregnated with Faith, what the Word of God says concerning our addictions or weaknesses, and know for certain that we will receive according to our Faith; that God has already blessed us with ALL spiritual blessings in heavenly places and on earth in Christ Jesus (Eph. 1.3).

Everything that we will ever need in this journey is provided by our Lord.  Prayer is the act of "walking by faith and not by sight," as Paul wrote in 2 Cor. 5.7). Knowing that God's Word is true and unchanging, we immediately apply it to our particular problem; we also know that the Word of God is Fact and not a feeling; nor is it the power of the intellect or an act of our will--- though we engage our intellect and will in a quality decision to act on the Word of God.

Faith comes by hearing, acknowledging and putting into practice the Word. It is not putting God to a foolish test when putting Him in remembrance of His promises. It's not that God forgets anything, but quoting His Word back to Him---or out loud in the earth---places a definite time for the fulfillment of that promise, for God who lives in eternity outside of time. We become the point of contact, being both an eternal and finite being where time and eternity meet within our Physical Body. Then God can and will answer the prayer, because He has our permission, our petition or request, the legal right to interfere in our life.

Faith declared, "I have it NOW! Hope declares, "I will have it!" Mental assent declares, "The Word states that I should have it but I don't see it!" Also, mental assent, which is basically human reasoning declares, "I must have sinned (again) and that's why I don't have my petition!"

Lasting Recovery involves genuine Faith; without Faith it is impossible to please God (Heb. 11.6). Do we fully grasp what the word "impossible" means? Neither does Hope please God, though it is the object of our Faith (what we want from God). And mental assent doesn't please God or move His hand to help us. All mental assent can do is think of reasons why the Word doesn't work for us, or why God is withholding His promises.

Mental assent is the mental processes without the input of the human spirit; it is actually the self-life maneuvering to get back on the throne of our life. As it stands, as Born Again Believers, Christ sits on the throne of our life and self is at His feet; the self wants to again be the ruler, with Christ setting at his feet, or out the door!

In the same way that Abraham was fully persuaded that God's promises and His oaths were realities, we must believe: Adhere to, trust in and rely on His promises and His ability and willingness to perform them admirably. This implies not considering the outer situations, circumstances or appearances. But give praise, worship and thanks to God BEFORE the results come, BEFORE the healing, BEFORE the deliverance, and BEFORE the finances arrive.

"Do not fret or have any anxiety about anything, but in every Circumstance and in everything, by prayer and petition (definite requests), with thanksgiving, continue to make your wants known to God. 7 And God's peace {shall be yours, that tranquil state of a soul assured of its salvation through Christ, and so fearing nothing from God...} which transcends all understanding shall garrison and mount guard over your hearts and minds in Christ Jesus" Phil. 4.6,7.

Faith is believing God's Word; Fear is believing Satan's word. Herein the key to receiving answered prayer: Faith and definite requests to God, believing that we have already received before we actually make the requests. Because we believe that God loves us and already answered our prayer, we rest assured in that tranquil state of praise and worship---fearing nothing that the demons may bring to slow down or stop our blessing---until we see the manifestation of our prayer.

Having peace that transcends all understanding, drives the demons out! Fearing nothing that comes our way in life is the results of Faith in God; living according to the Word of God goes hand-in-hand with Faith. We cannot have genuine Faith in God and not adhere to, trust in and rely on His revealed Word. Knowing that God cares for us lovingly, affectionately, and watchfully makes it easier to go to Him for Forgiveness, Inner Healing and Deliverance.

Most of us wouldn't confess to anyone we believe would kill us when we are done. And that is what the Devil wants us to think about God. So he tells us to hide our sins, suppress or hide our addictions, indulgences, urges and thinking distortions instead of getting help.

Then one day he springs the trap and the whole world knows what we have been doing more or less all of our life! Jos. 1.8 advises us not to let the Word of God depart from our mouth; and the only way it will be in the mouth is that it first be abundantly in the heart; for out of the abundance of the heart {human spirit's intuition, intellect, emotions, will, imagination} the mouth will speak. Then we'll experience soul prosperity. Praying according to the Word, which is hidden in our heart, keeps us from habitual sin.

Another great principle to consider is written in Mat. 18.18 (Amp. Bible). "Truly I tell you, whatever you forbid and declare to be improper and unlawful on earth must be what is already forbidden in heaven, and whatever you permit and declare proper and lawful on earth must be what is already permitted in heaven."

The Standard for what is unlawful or improper is in relation to the Word of God. Evil, the entire works of Satan has been declared unlawful everywhere except in Hell. When we pray the perfect will of God "Thy will be done in earth as it is in heaven," we are requesting that the same Standard be invoked here on earth that is the Spiritual Law and legal state environment in Heaven. For example: There is no sicknesses, diseases, addictions or criminal activity in heaven, and so we can declare and decree ourselves legally free (as the fruit of Salvation) of all of these bondages on earth.

And the second part of the verse affirms the legal status of Heaven with our free will to declare and decree freedom according to the Spiritual Law of the Spirit of Life, the legal state of Heaven that is free from evil and its consequences. For whom the Son of God has set free is free indeed!

Addictions know no boundaries: Age, race, gender, social status, the Saved and un-Saved fall victim to drugs, alcohol, tobacco, sexual addictions, and deviant, antisocial behaviors. However, we as Christians have a resource available that others do not have: A Covenant relationship with God. It is a matter of if we want to remain a Victim or achieve Victory. Because God can turn a mess into a message, a test into a testimony, a trial into a triumph, and a victim into a victory.

Sometimes we think that God is going to do everything for us, that He can somehow "force us" to follow the Word. But that is not the truth. God did not force us to get Saved nor will He force us to stay Saved. God, through Jesus Christ and the Holy Spirit are Covenant Partners with us. As Partners, the Trinity will not and cannot do all of the work; we have to purposely engage our will and cooperate with our Partners. And as the Three are One in Spirit, we don't have to satisfy three different Persons, but One. Nevertheless, we pray to the Father in Jesus' Name because He told us too.

Mat. 18.19 (Amp. Bible) concludes and establishes that the action must began with us, on earth, and not in Heaven at the throne of God: "Again I tell you, if two of you on earth agree (harmonize together, make a symphony together) about whatever {anything and every-thing} they may ask, it will come to pass and be done for them by My Father in heaven." Two Christians in agreement can turn the table on the Devil and erase a multitude of sins.

Herein lies the authority and power of the Believer to destroy yokes and lift heavy burdens. Hiding our sins isn't the answer; it is like a closet full of filthy clothes that as time passes stinks up the whole house; or worst, a refrigerator, that has been turned off for months but full of raw meat, then opened! Getting sins forgiven, washed away and their outworking consequences made none and void is the ideal goal.

Therefore, we come into agreement with one another, bind the demonic spirits responsible for the sicknesses or addictions on earth, and God in Heaven honors our decisions and causes them to be tangible in our life.

God knows what we have need of before we ask; nevertheless, we ask that He may enter into our life. Ask and you shall receive, is what Jesus taught; also, have Faith in God, or have the Faith of

God by speaking positive words of Faith, and call those things that be not as yet as though they already exist in the natural realm. Walking by Faith and not by sight is what we are talking about. If we believe that God's Word is true we have to live by it.

This will cause our Faith to grow from the mustard seed kind to the great Faith that Jesus spoke of concerning the Roman centurion. Though everyone has been dealt a measure of Faith in order to get Saved in the first place, not everyone uses their Faith to get Saved, but use it to follow other religions and philosophies; but Faith increases by hearing, acknowledging and putting into practice the Word of God.

Fear creates doubt: Doubt comes by hearing and practicing unbelief, false religions and philosophies. So we have to practice being positive in our thinking and don't give up on ourselves or recovery. This is done by praying the solution and not complaining to God, ourselves or to friends about the problem. Every thought or action must mirror and confirm what we believe God for. Being vigilant, lest a negative mental image of failure stay in the conscious mind too long and become a permanent fixture! If doubt, which is a vain imagination comes into the mind, rebuke it, and it will burst like a bubble. Summit to God, resist the Devil and he will flee (Jam. 4.7).

"Because when they knew and recognized Him as God, they did not honor and glorify Him as God or give Him thanks. But instead they became futile and godless in their thinking {with vain imagining, foolish reasoning and stupid speculations} and their senseless minds were darkened. 22 Claiming to be wise, they became fools..." ---Ro. 1.21,22.

The imagination is the facility of the soul that is capable of conceiving and grasping abstract ideas, concepts, theories and principles. It enables us to plan today for a possible tomorrow (which is not promised to any of us). The imagination is also the facility of the soul that can create art, literature, music, build and construct things that have never existed before; it is also the facility that we use to dream at night, daydream or fantasize.

But imagination corrupted by the flesh, world or demons, becomes the facility used to create paranoia—fearful, terrifying and paralyzing thoughts that people are after us to do harm when they are not; it also creates doubt, unbelief, religious error, racism, sexual fantasy, lust, pride, vanity, self-importance and self-righteousness; these are examples of vain imaginations.

Vain imaginations are often projected into our minds by the territorial spirits; often it is done during the sleep state, meditations or daydreaming period when the mind is idle and open. Certain Eastern meditation techniques relax the mind as to become vulnerable to psychic attacks from demons.

God has imagination too; His is called divine imaginations. Through His facility He sends us what we call visions and dreams. This is one of God's primary methods of communication. Divine imaginations is God sending us mental images (pictures) of our future or visual information about others; He also sends us visual information about local or world situations and circumstances, our destiny and Calling, His plans, purposes and pursuits using us or just the overall plan; He also sends visions of Himself so that we can personally know Him.

The mind of God is like a television station. He sends out powerful visual images with an audible tract containing information about who He is, and His plans. These images may be real time or future; and since God always is in the present, He knows what is destined to happen throughout human history. Those who are sensitive and close to God see visions from God; God is no respecter of persons; He will talk to anyone who will listen to what He has to say!

"Be well balanced (temperate, sober of mind), be vigilant and cautious at all times; for that enemy of yours, the devil, roams around like a lion roaring {in fierce hunger}, seeking someone to seize upon and devour. 9 Withstand him; be firm in faith…"1 Pet. 5.8,9.

The biggest deception that Satan has pulled off since the Garden of Eden is to convince humanity that he doesn't exist. The Word of God declares that there is such a person as Satan or the Devil, and that he is alive and living on Earth. He is not as powerful as he was before Calvary, since the decisive victory won by Jesus Christ, but he still remains the most notorious murderer, liar and trickster that has even lived. But those who are In Christ Jesus, have weapons to fight against this entity. Knowing this, we are not ignorant of his devices and tactics.

Satan moves and maneuvers in the Psychic or Mental Realm, the realm of the senses; he also uses subtle suggestions, deceptions and delusions. One thing for sure, his implanted thoughts do not line up with the Word of God and can be easily discerned by those of us who diligently study the Bible. But, during the years when we didn't know the Word of God, was when Satan got his foothold.

Now we have to be more conscious of our thought processes, motives, desires and reasoning to make sure we are not being lured into one of his traps. We have to cast down and reject dreams, visions, false prophecies or personal feelings that don't line up with the Word. We also have to practice resisting the "doubting Thomas'" of the local churches and the world.

As doubting Thomas' we sound so knowledgeable when we say: "Once an alcoholic, always an alcoholic, or "Once a drug addict, always a drug addict"---which is NOT the Word of God concerning New Creatures in Christ Jesus; this thinking distortion is also extended to other moral failures as a reason not to help fallen Christians get back on their feet; it is also proclaiming that the Blood of Jesus Christ is powerless to deliver addicts or certain people, therefore doubting the effectiveness of the Word of God. And so we would rather use this excuse to shoot the fallen Christians like injured horses!

Jesus Christ took upon Himself our grief, sicknesses, weaknesses and distresses, even the pains and conse-quences of punishment, and with the stripes that wounded Him we are healed and made whole (Isa. 53.4). In so doing, He not only secured eternal Salvation for those who believe in him, but Healing and Deliverance from the molestation of unclean spirits.

That is why the weapons of our warfare are not physical weapons, but mighty and effective to demolish strong-holds of every kind; there is no bondage that the Holy Spirit cannot break; and the only person that He cannot save is the one who doesn't want to get Saved. For the most part, thoughts are formed in the brain by observation, association, and teaching.

Though it is difficult to avoid hearing other people's opinions, we can nevertheless avoid soul ties with them, certain places, programs and reading printed materials that is contrary to Christian belief, that doesn't support our confession of Faith, Healing and Deliverance.

Face it, if we want to stop drinking we have to stop buying liquor, going to bars and clubs and hanging out with people who drink! Why? Because we are saying one thing and doing another; we are not making arrangements to  stop  but to continue drink-ing.  This principle applies to all addictions, strongholds, habits or thinking distortions: Feed your Faith and starve your Doubts to death! Whatever you feed will get the fattest; whatever you starve will eventually die.

Thinking positively is not a new idea. Non-Christian motivational speakers have capitalized on this concept, and perhaps have helped a lot of depressed people; they have also created a lot of multimillion and billionaires too. But positive thinking alone will not change the core of us, though it will alter many thinking patterns.

Here is where the Word of God and prayer comes in, the help of the powerful, life-changing Holy Spirit. Not letting the Word depart from before our eyes and heart is the key to confessing the truth in the earth about who we are, and the positive confession of our destiny with our mouth. And God will make His Word good if we diligently act upon it.

We make every prayer a confession of Faith, and don't undo those prayers by listening to the "speculations," the vain imaginations of our mind whose goal is to return to the familiar, that former state of pleasure and freedom from God, that state of thinking that it's okay to sin as long as it's temporary; or, "I'm Saved, so I can sin and not lose my Salvation… or I am the Bishop, and so…"

We pray to the Father in the Name of Jesus (Jn. 16.23); there isn't another way to approach God and be accepted by Him. Because of our confidence in Jesus, the Father answers and grants our petitions. Our praying authority comes from Jesus, the High Priest of the Heavenly Sanctuary (Acts 3.12). Without the use of His Name, we are stuck, like other religions, with a form of godliness without the actual relationship and power to overcome adversity---mainly, our adversary the Devil, and our wicked desires to please our flesh. Prayer is planting the seed of Faith to claim our harvest!

notes

# Chapter Two

## Types of Prayers

There are many types of prayers and ways to pray; since this is not a book on prayer alone, we will only discuss a few types.

**The Prayer of Faith** is described in many ways and places in the New Testament. Prayer for the Christian is based on the New Testament Covenant. We should not pray like David prayed under the Old Testament Covenant of Law--- that God would kill our enemies. But under Grace there is forgiveness and mercy.

In Mk. 11.24 it states, "Therefore I tell you, whatever you ask for in prayer, believe that you have received it, and it will be yours." Jesus proclaimed, "Have Faith in God." Another translation says, "Have the Faith of God," which also makes sense because God does everything through the exercise of His Faith. He has dealt to everyone a measure, a degree, a mustard seed of His divine Faith. God, through Faith, calls those things that be not as though they already were; this is the Prayer based and rooted in Faith---to call those things that be not as yet as though they already exist.

In Eph. 6.10-17, the Apostle Paul gave a discourse on spiritual warfare. From there he immediately wrote of prayer being an essential part of that spiritual warfare: "Pray at all times (on every occasion, in every season) in the Spirit, with all {manner of} prayer and entreaty" Eph 6.18 (Amp).

**The Prayer of Consecration** is another type of prayer that is widely described and used in the New Testament Covenant. To consecrate means to sanctify, separate for a divine purpose. We as Christians are a people set aside by God. We are members of

His divine family, the Church, the Bride of Christ, the fruit, being the children of the Resurrection.

Therefore, we are separated from the world, and do separate ourselves by uttering this type of prayer. We declare and decree aloud that we belong to Christ and He belongs to us! In the upper room, Jesus consecrated the wine and the bread through prayer. "And as they were eating, Jesus took bread, and blessed it, and brake it, and gave it to the disciples, and said, "Take, eat, this is my body. And He took the cup, and gave thanks, and gave it to them, saying, Drink ye all of it.

For this is my blood of the New Testament" (Mat. 28.26-28). In Jn. 17.15-17 (Amp. Bible), Jesus consecrated, set apart disciples for a special purpose: "I do not ask that You take them out of the world, but that You will keep and protect them from the evil one. They are not of the world (worldly, belonging to the world), {just} as I am not of the world. Sanctify them {purify, consecrate, separate them for Yourself, make them holy} by the Truth; Your word is Truth."

In further verses, Jesus consecrated Him-self and future Believers in the Body of Christ, so that we are also sanctified, purified, separated and wholly consecrated to and In Him. In the same way the Father sent Jesus into the world, Jesus sends us into the world with the same consecration through prayer.

**Prayer of Commitment:** "Delight your-self also in the Lord, and He will give you the desires and secret petitions of your heart. Commit your ways to the Lord {roll and repose each care of your load on Him}; trust (lean on, rely on, and be confident) also in Him and He will bring it to pass" (Ps. 37.4,5 Amp. Bible).

It is obvious that the Prayer of Commitment involves our spiritual relationship with God. It is our commitment to Him, not His commitment to us that is involved. God is faithful; and we are not always faithful, though we try with all our might. Many times are burdens are so heavy that we cannot lift them; that is when we roll or drag them to the cross.

Then there are times when out burdens are so heavy that we have not the strength to roll or drag them; that is when we seek out a prayer partner, a Christian to stand in agreement and believe with us, that what we ask, believing that we have already received, will materialize according to our Faith in the Word of God. Peter wrote, "Casting the whole of your cares {all you anxieties, all your worries. All your concerns, once and for all} on Him; for He cares for you affectionately and cares about you watchfully" (1 Pet. 5.7 Amp. Bible).

This is saying a lot about our New Testament Covenant; how God is available and willing to accept our burdens as His own and either help us to carry them or eliminate them altogether. Prayer is the key to getting supernatural help in this natural world; having God in our world when the world is more or less Godless. Jesus affirmed this when speaking to the disciples concerning the Battle of Life: "Therefore I say to you, do not worry about your life, what you will eat; or about your body, what you will wear. But seek His kingdom, and these things will be given to you as well" (Lk. 12.22,31).

Knowing this truth frees us from the anxiety (fear) of worrying about finances, health, marriage and the host of other concerns we have as human being living in a materialistic world. God knows that we don't live in a cave; He knows we need a certain amount of money to survive on, and so He says commit our ways to Him and he will take care of us.

### Praying In Tongues

"For he that speaks in an unknown tongue, speaks not unto men, but unto God; for no man understands him, howbeit in the Spirit he speaks mysteries. 1 "But you, beloved, building up yourself on your most holy faith, praying in the Holy Ghost" ---1 Cor. 14.4; Jude 1.20.

Praying in Tongues is the last type of prayer to be discussed in this chapter. This phenomenon is strictly a New Testament manifestation of the Holy Spirit. Over the years there has been much controversy concerning the Baptism in/with the Holy Spirit, accompanied by the scriptural evidence of speaking in other/ unknown tongues (Acts.2.4).

**The Baptism in the Holy Spirit** is a second work of Grace through Faith. It was made possible for Believers to receive this gift on the day of Pentecost---fifty days after the crucifixion of the Lord Jesus Christ. Further evidence that we have been Baptized in the Holy Spirit is the manifestation of one or several of the nine Spiritual Gifts: Tongues, Interpretation of Tongues, Discerning of Spirits, Prophecy, Word of Wisdom, Word of Knowledge, Gifts of Healing, Working of Miracles, and the Gift of Faith (1 Cor. 12.7-11).

The difference between the Baptism in the Holy Spirit and Salvation, is that Salvation/Regeneration involves the indwelling and residence of the Holy Spirit within our human spirit causing a spiritual awakening and Eternal Life; whereas, the Baptism in the Holy Spirit is power for service.

We can be Saved without the Baptism in the Holy Spirit; but we cannot be un-Saved and Baptized in the Holy Spirit. In order to qualify to receive the second work of Grace, the first work of Grace, Salvation must be accomplished. There are many New Testament examples where the Believer received both apparently at the same time; but in the Word of God, Salvation took first place even if it was only by a second.

The manifestations of Spiritual Gifts is not a sign of biblical knowledge, integrity, good character, morals or superiority; it is only that God---who is no respecter of persons---chose us as a vessel to accomplish some task for Him; and He did the choosing before the foundation of the world.

The benefits to those of us Christians who are Baptized in the Holy Spirit is our increased power and awareness of who we are in Christ, and our ability to talk to the Father, Son or Holy Spirit, and speak mysteries into the natural world, in a language that cannot be twisted or corrupted by our flesh, unclean spirits that may be hidden deep within our soul (intellect, emotions, will, imagination), or those assigned to curse, hinder, tempt, destroy or monitor us.

Unclean spirits can create delusions and a blocking action to keep us from asking or receiving the help of God. They can deceive us into thinking that we are okay, and the Word concerning the renewing of the mind is for other Christians who need it more than we do, that everyone else is wrong; it also can be we are led to believe that no one will ever discover what we are doing.

But praying in the Spirit is supernatural and the territorial spirits or indwelling spirits don't know what we are praying about (they lost their ability to interpret this spiritual language). But in our daily dialect---since demons have been on the earth prior to the Garden of Eden---they can understand and fluently speak every language that was ever spoken on earth; but they cannot interpret the Language of the Spirit of Life, the "original" language of God and the holy angels.

Apostle Paul and Apostle Jude wrote that speaking in tongues edifies, builds us up spiritually (1 Cor. 14.4  Jude 1.20). There is yoke-destroying, devil-stomping power in praying in Tongues. "For if I pray in an unknown tongue, my spirit prays, but my understanding is unfruitful" (1 Cor. 14.14). This states that we are strengthened and build up where we are weak, but this is done independently of the intellect, emotions, will and imagination; it cannot be influenced by us or the demonic powers.

This is available power for living in Christ. The speaking in Tongues is the Holy Spirit talking or praying from His residence in us. And though we are Saved without this Baptism, and have the Person of the Holy Spirit in us, He has not been given our permission to use our mouth to speak into our life, and to speak the perfect will of God into the earth.

We gave Him permission to indwell us and live, but not permission to speak out of our mouth the perfect will of God as He deems (not us) necessary, and at His appropriate timing. This is something to seriously think about!

The Baptism in the Holy Spirit is vital to getting set free on the inside and outside---declaring the Word of God, decreeing the Word of God, and taking spiritual authority through the Word of God by praying in the Holy Spirit.

The Baptism in the Holy Spirit tongues can also be prayed corporately, that is, the entire church can pray aloud together (This is not preaching in Tongues which is forbid-den because no one knows what is being said); or the Gift of Tongues can be uttered as long as someone immediately interprets it (1 Cor. 14).

The Baptism in the Holy Spirit is a must for Christians to fight a winning Battle of Life and For Life. How do we as Christians get Baptized in the Holy Spirit? Here is a clue: John the Baptist declared: "But He that sent me to baptize with water, the same said unto me. Upon whom you shall see the Spirit descending, and remain on Him, the same is He which baptizes with the Holy Ghost" (Jn. 1.33). So we see through scriptural reference, the Person John was referring to is Jesus Christ; He is the One who Baptizes us in the Holy Spirit, for He is also the one who sent the Holy Spirit back to the natural realm to continue His work of Redemption. The Baptism in the Holy Spirit, a gift received by Faith, can be received by direct prayer or laying on of hands by any Christian who is also Baptized in the Holy Spirit. Often, after Inner Healing and Deliverance has taken place, the Baptism in the Holy Spirit is easier to receive.

## Deliverance Prayer

Heavenly Father, I humble myself before You in the Name of Jesus Christ. I confess my sins; I am sorry for every one of them. I have accepted Jesus Christ as my Lord and Savior.

I am redeemed by the Blood of Jesus and accept Forgiveness Inner Healing and Deliverance.

Lord, through the power of the Holy Spirit, completely cleanse me. I have unwisely allowed (Name the unclean spirit(s) to gain access, oppress, torment and use me.

I seek to recover my freedom, wholeness, and to exercise free will over my spirit, soul, mental facilities, will, intellect, emotions, imagination and physical body, to be set free of all infirmities and influences of unclean spirits.

I denounce Satan and his plans, purposes, and pursuits. I separate myself from Satan and claim refuge in the Lord Jesus Christ. I demand and decree my immediate release from all evil spirits and influences operating in my life.

In Jesus' Name, I exercise my will and Christian Authority over evil spirits assigned to harass, steal, kill and destroy me.

I bind and break your power, strongholds, thinking distortions, delusions, addictions and influences in the Name of Jesus.

**BY NOW FAITH**: In the Name of Jesus Christ, I NOW declare that you unclean spirits are unlawfully encroaching according to the Word of God: I demand that you leave me! I am a child of God. I declare: Depart from me you cursed spirits!

**BY NOW FAITH**: I claim the promises: (Joel 2.32) "That whosoever shall call upon the Name of the Lord shall be delivered." The Word cleanses me from all sin. I am a holy temple of God; and Greater is He within me than he that is in the world.

I belong to Christ and Him only will I serve. Lord Jesus Christ, right NOW, I accept my Deliverance. Fill me, Lord, with your Holy Spirit. Bless the Name of Jesus. Amen!

### Prayer Of Dominion

Father, in the Name of Jesus, I take spiritual authority against the Principalities, Powers, Rulers of the Darkness and Spiritual Wickedness in the heavenly places assigned to this region.

I exercise dominion against all demonic manipulations, control, influences and strongholds.

I declare them to be unlawfully assembled according to the Word of God. Therefore in the Name and by the Blood of Jesus, I render their works bound in the earth as they are in Heaven. In Jesus' Name, I openly declare that every manifestation, operation, assignment or maneuver of the enemy has become ineffective and made void.

I exercise dominion against all evil spirits assigned to steal, kill and destroy this people. In the Name and by the Blood of Jesus Christ, I bind all unclean spirits, including tormenting, perversion, lying, prejudice, racism, anger, hatred, unforgiveness, rebellion, religion, legalism, condemnation, guilt, inferiority, rejection, greed, drug dealing, drug and alcohol addictions, violence, child abuse, domestic violence, pornography, sexual perversions, sin, sicknesses, diseases, poverty---plus every spirit that binds and oppresses this people.

**BY NOW FAITH**, I activate the Blood of Jesus over this region and over this people. I declare the Blood to be a witness against the territorial spirit activity and their eternal defeat. I now release this people in the Name of Jesus from all bondages and pronounce them free to serve the Lord Jesus Christ.

**BY NOW FAITH**, I declare the people blessed and open to the Spirit of God, sensitive to the voice of the Holy Spirit, the Word and the will of God.

I decree that where sin abounds that Grace much more abounds, that the Life and Light of Christ prevails against the darkness of Satan, that truth prevails against deception; Deliverance prevails against bondage, and obedience prevails against rebellion.

Father, I thank and praise You that Your Kingdom has come and Your will is being done in the earth as it is in Heaven.

I declare in the Name of Jesus that this region is holy ground and consecrated to Your purpose. Holy Spirit, fall upon this region and make Your Presence known, that the will of God be enforced by the Church. To Jesus be honor and glory forever, amen.

Notes

# Chapter Three

## Time-Wasters & Haters.

"And he shall speak great words against the Most High, and shall ware out the saints of the Most High"--- Dan. 7.25.

These are undoubtedly the years of Restitution and New Beginnings. Those who embrace this paradigm shift that has taken place in the Spirit Realm must be particularly careful as not to allow the enemy to steal our time!  We all, being mortals, have a certain amount of time to live, and therefore a limited amount of time to do what God has called us to do.

Satan and the territorial spirits will attempt to persuade us to invest our limited time and resources in the sensual world of pleasure, entertainment and other worldly endeavors, and not be Born Again, or enter into our appointed destiny, and subsequently not finish the course with joy.

Time is our valuable asset; seasons are window opportunities placed in time. If we miss the time we also miss the season. Satan's end time strategy is to wear out the saints of God. Since he was defeated by Jesus Christ at Calvary, his strategy is to mentally and physically wear us out through futile behaviors, wasted motions and fleshly acts of service---be they religious or secular.

The motive is to scatter our attention from the true plan and purpose of God in our life and waste precious time, whereby we leave out of this world tired, worn out, disappointed, disgusted, unsatisfied and defeated.

Time Wasters are demon spirits that hate us and use people to impede out spiritual progress; they but they create and operate through distractions. Distractions manifest as people, events, situations and circumstances that take our focus off of Christ, the Christian Purpose and destiny that God has predestined, prepared and appointed us for.

In the **Battle For Life**, we have to be careful if we are to acquire and maintain our Inner Healing and Deliverance; there are haters among us---servants of the Time-Wasting spirits.

Even in the local churches are many Haters; we all know this group or class of Christian---people who don't want to see us prosper. If it were advantageous to plan a Hater's Convention, the extraordinary task would be to find a building large enough to hold so many Haters; or perhaps a large island should be leased? Then, there is always the possibility that no one would come to the Hater's Convention because they hate each other too!

**The Haters** are the Christian Soldiers who shoot to death their own wounded comrades; who will not lift a finger to support a fallen brother, sister or pastor, but are quick to stand over us and administer the coup de grace. Beware of them: They are one of the most lethal weapons in Satan's arsenal.

When we are enjoying our peace and recovery from drugs, alcohol or a sexual morality fall, here they come to forever  hold our failure (s) over our head,  saying "I am so disappointed in you---how could you have done such a thing! I will never trust you again!" They are Time Wasters.

Other examples of Time Wasters are **Excessive** conventions, board meetings, committees, office parties, sororities, frats, lodges, clubs, functions, toxic relationships, soul ties, arguing, procrastination, family dysfunctions, church programs, drifting from church-to-church, compulsive prophecy hunting, reliving past traumas, all grudges, isolation, rebellion against church leaders, talking, gossip, eating, recreation, vacations, entertainment, social networks, video games, workaholic, love of the world, money, gambling, alcohol, drugs, all sexual immorality, politics for power, non-Christian conventions and meetings, all practicing of non-Christian doctrines, societies (like Eastern Star Masons) and philosophies, avoiding Counseling or Inner Healing & Deliverance when needed.

There are endless ways to waste our precious time her on earth. A cause that appears on the surface to be good, necessary and noble, could actually tie us up and keep us from being used by God, when the position could be adequately filled by someone who doesn't want to serve God but is interested in politics and public service.

Sometimes, a spirit of "false burden" leads us (deceives us by playing on our emotions, feelings or sense of wanting to see change) to believe that no one can do the job but us; we must sit on the committee at the school board, hospital, city council or even a church-run board. But if after consulting God we do not receive the "go"---leave it alone; for us, it is a Time Waster, though it may be a legitimate cause and worthy of being done--- but not by us! We must redeem the times because the days are numbered and extremely evil.

## The Undiscovered Country

The Undiscovered Country is similar to the new world that the Europeans arrived in during the 1600s. They risked their lives to venture to the new world, and many of them were buried during the harsh winter. But as soon as the winter was over, they pressed further inland to discover the rest of the country.

The Undiscovered Country is that territory within us that we have not known, neither have we explored; for we have not come this way before. The Undiscovered Country is also the New Creature in Christ Jesus, the part of us whom we have to be acquainted with, embrace, love, obey and appreciate, though we know a whole lot about the old creature.

Many philosophers have expounded on this concept by proclaiming, "Know Thyself! Some refer to the old creature we were as the dark side of the soul, or the part of all of us we keep hidden out of sight, suppressed and under lock and key, less he gets out publicly and ruins our entire life. And so, we wear all types of masks and costumes because life is a Broadway production. Therefore, in order to know thyself we have to study thyself in light of what the Word of God says.

The Undiscovered Country is the part of us that if there was no law or punishment for wrongdoing, we would do almost anything! It is our deepest, darkest, best-kept secrets that if anyone found out, they would be appalled. It is that part of us that even God said was desperately wicked. In counseling those incarcerated in prison, it was discovered that the majority of those convicted of heinous crimes including serial murders, never thought that they were capable of such acts.

Even their family members, neighbors and school teachers were shocked to hear of the news. "He is so polite!" Some said, "He is so quiet!" Others said. "He was in church every Sunday," The pastor added. But, of course, they were wrong about what was in that person's heart. We should never say what we will not do; if it were not for the Grace of God that we are in our right mind (some of us) we would be in prison, a mental institution, homeless or on Death Row with the hundreds of men and women exhausting appeals or awaiting execution.

And so it is with the Christians who have fallen. What is needed most is we that are spiritual to help them get back on their feet--- not to constantly remind them of the fall, and burn the forever brand on the forehead: SINNER! And more often than not the church aligns in agreement with the world and not the Word of God concerning Repentance and Faith.

The world does not believe that fallen people can permanently change because repentance or the "Born Again" experience. It is interesting how certain Christians, the Haters believe that the Blood of Jesus Christ is capable of taking away their sins but not anyone else's sins. It is the double standard in the local church. This type of thinking devalues the Blood of Jesus, and groups it with other religious "phrases."

When we ask a Christian, "How are you doing?" The usual response is, "Blessed." Which is eternally true, but doesn't provide us any useful information to get to know them. They are wearing the "Christian Mask," pretending that they have no problems, struggles, or need prayer or wise counsel for anything.

The devaluing of the power of the Blood causes us to discount the Blood as Atonement for sins of the fallen Christian. The exercise of Faith necessary to invoke the release of cleansing, does not happen because the Blood of Jesus has become a mental and religious concept, and not a Faith-based reality.

Therefore, many churches have stopped singing songs about the Blood of Jesus because it sounds gross to them (the Blood being made common as human or animal blood). So when Christians fall, the response is ridicule, separation or excommunication, "silencing" as the Baptists call it. But God, who knows and is the Way, Truth, and Life said:

"The heart is deceitful above all things, and it is exceedingly perverse and corrupt and severely, mortally sick! Who can know it {perceive, understand, be acquainted with his own heart and mind}"---Jer. 19.9.

The King James Version describes the heart as "desperately wicked." The idea is the same: Without the Grace and help of God we might do anything!

The Undiscovered Country is also the place where demonic spirits hide. They hide here because it is the least likely place for us to perceive or be aware of their presence. From the comfortable council room, they pull the strings that make us jump and do weird things---that please them. So, we have to be aware of Seemingly Unimportant Decisions (SUD).

When we are not using our minds, being passive or practicing Transcendental Meditation, Yoga, or other Eastern "enlightening" disciplines, we are more open to suggestions than we were if we were using the functions of our mind. When we empty the mind of relevant thoughts and feelings, or cease to monitor our thoughts, feelings and emotions, we enter into the Undiscovered Country.

And like the "default" setting and subprogram on a computer that returns when it has lost track of what it is doing, we return and lean on the familiar arm of the flesh; there, the demons are waiting to get control of our life; and the SUD thought is likely the one that leads us in the direction to sin; because it will be the one that come out of us so powerfully; nevertheless, we will know it for what it is because it will NEVER pass the test of the Word of God!

Many people have fallen into sin because of that Seemingly Unimportant Decision. It could be visiting an ex-girlfriend when one or both people are married; or going to the store in the middle of the night and get robbed! On that note, thousands of people are in prison because of the sudden urge to go someplace or do something uncharacteristic of them and weird.

## Vain Imaginations

"Casting down imaginations…and bringing into captivity every thought to the obedience of Christ"---2Cor. 10.5.

Thoughts + Feelings +Emotions = Behaviors. As stated earlier, there  is such a thing as the imagination being out of phase with the rest of the mind, including the intellect. A Christian must guard against recurring thoughts that belong to the old man or demons, who will use these thoughts to regain his former position; and the spirits that are associated with the old man will definitely use the flesh, the self-life and the Law of Sin and Death to regain control. Below are but a few vain imaginations and thoughts to consider:

I deserve better.
I feel insecure.
Others are ahead of me.
What's wrong with me?
I'm a loser.
I feel inadequate.
I want revenge.
People are out to get me.
God has forgotten me!
I'm not as spiritual as others.
I'm slow and stupid.
No one likes me.
I shouldn't even try.
I will only fail.
Why is this happening to me?
I'm always wrong.
It's my parent's fault.
I deserve to feel sorry for myself.

My anger doesn't hurt anyone.
Using alcohol and drugs helps me.

## Feelings & Emotions

Inadequacy, insecurity, boredom, Condemnation, hopelessness, low self-esteem, jealousy, embarrassment   Impatience, blame others, defective   Worried, confused, rejection, anxiety   shame, guilt, weird, victim, envy, stress, strange, guilt, fear,

## Behaviors

Anger and rage directed towards self and others, murder, violence directed towards people and property, severe assaults, drug and alcohol use and abuse, criminal acts (felonies) juvenile delinquency,  setting fires (arson) torturing or killing animals,  sexual fantasies, sexual assault, lying, denial,  arguing, cursing, intimidation, closed mind,  obsessive, religious rituals, deviant behaviors, lack of  trust, lust, pride, lasciviousness, sarcasm, looking depressed, spaced out, excessive compulsiveness, unusually quiet, clenched fist, unnecessary body tension.

## Demonic Interference

Although there are hundreds of symptoms of demonic interference, some of which have their root in emotional and medical disorders that may be chemical or electrical related, a physician should always be consulted. As these lists are only a guide-line to recognizing problems, it is not meant to be conclusive or a substitute for medical attention.

Failure to get breakthrough after days of fasting and prayers. Unexplained illness with no diagnosis, including rashes. Practicing the Occult (including witchcraft, Tara Cards, Voodoo and Ouija board). Repeated backsliding in the same area. Chronic depression, suicide attempts, hostile behavior, unexplained sulfur-like odor, seizures, suddenly  compelled to go places, cutting the flesh, excessive compulsive behaviors, difficulty reading Bible, difficulty worshipping, difficulty repenting, mental illnesses (all types), hearing voices, mocking the Word of God, cursing God or Jesus, superhuman strength terror in the mind, recurring nightmares, flashbacks, seeing evil spirits, claims to be a reincarnation, actual visitation by evil spirits.

Jesus is the Great Physician. He said, "Ask and you shall receive. It is always to our best interest to do what Jesus says. But often times, we find it all but impossible to obey His Word. These are times when the influences of the demonic kingdom, family, friends and religious folks are at their worst in our lives.

It is beneficial to our spiritual growth to be find a trusted, dedicated, non-judgmental professional to get help; a ministry empowered by the Holy Spirit and devoted to setting the captives free, is what's needed; not a gossiper or busybody. We should pray and ask God to direct us to someone whom He uses to release and activate Physical Healing, Emotional Healing, Deliverance and Restoration.

### Why do you seek Healing & Deliverance?

We as Christians are required to live by the Standard of the Word of God. The Christian denominations, the Constitution and legal system even adds a little more to that. Christians are to live a life above reproach and blame.

Many of us strive daily to live up to these standards; sometimes we are trusting in God, other times we are maintaining a façade, the appearance of living holy---going through the motions---when in fact we are only suppressing the manifestations of our urges, fantasies and desires. But even the smallest volcano will someday blow, and the destruction in its wake can be most devastating to those around it.

The Undiscovered Country is full of active and dormant volcanoes: Some small and others humongous. Many have erupted and spent their fury and now lain dormant. But there are many more potential disasters lurking deep below the surface. Under the right conditions they will bust loose with a fury that would be impossible for us to contain; impatience turns into irritation; irritation into anger; anger into rage; rage into violence; violence into murder; murder into imprisonment; imprisonment into State Execution.

Secret sins are not volcanoes but the effect are the same. Those urges that we suppress, fail to suppress and indulge in behind closed doors will be discovered. Below are a few "volcanoes" and manifestations of demonic activity. Some are already listed in the other categories:

Fear, worry, sickness and disease, chronic pain, Crack/cocaine/ heroin, prescription drug addiction, Marijuana, cigarettes, psychological addictions, gambling,  rejection,  rebellion, guilt, shame,  pride, stress, bitterness, jealousy, violence, road rage, criminality, stealing, overeating, laziness, procrastination, cursing, suicide, self hatred, lust abandonment, depression,  obsession;

emotional abuse, physical abuse, sexual abuse, incest, abortion, fornication, adultery, pornography, homosexuality, Lesbianism, Pedophilia, masturbation, fetishes, necrophilia, bestiality, forget-fulness, curses, hearing voices mental illness, paranoia, hatred of men,  hatred of women, spousal abuse, domestic violence, wit-chcraft, demonic interference, cults, religious error, can't find or keep employment, problems concentrating, or can't solve basic social problems.

The Undiscovered Country can be a very crowded place, a place that we seldom visit to clean house, but the occupants seem to come and go as they please! This is the place the Holy Spirit goes in and cleans house; He heals the hurts and soothes the pains; this is where He restores the fractured or fragmented personality---having been wounded during the Battle of Life and **The Battle For Life**.

Our personality was fractured by our own sins and lifestyle plus the deeds of familiar and territorial spirits. This was also added to by family and social pressures, abuse and betrayals; this is where the Love of Christ rushes in like a mighty wind and sweeps away the entrenched spirits who have been dictating to us their will and sometimes even our will---because, at times, we enjoyed sinning!

Even in a court of law, "the devil made me do it," Is not an accepted defense! We are responsible to God for the vain imaginations that lead us into actions that jeopardize our entire being; spirit, soul, natural body, and freedom, even though we may have been coerced to do evil.

### U.S. Prison Population Tops 2 Million

America's prison population topped 2 million inmates for the first time in history on June 30, 2002 according to a new report from the Justice Department's Bureau of Justice Statistics (BJS).

The 50 states, the District of Columbia and the federal government held 1,355,748 prisoners (two-thirds of the total incarcerated population), and local municipal and county jails held 665,475 inmates. By midyear 2002, America's jails held 1 in every 142 U.S. residents. Males were incarcerated at the rate of 1,309 inmates per 100,000 U.S. men, while the female incarceration rate was 113 per 100,000 women residents.

Of the 1,200,203 state prisoners, 3,055 were younger than 18 years old. In addition, adult jails held 7,248 inmates under 18. State and federal correctional authorities held 88,776 non-citizens. And a conservative estimate of those incarcerated worldwide is 9 million souls; this includes the innocent, persecuted Christians, political prisoners and mental institutions to allocated to "silence the opposition." America leads the world in freedoms, but also leads the world in criminals.

The legacy of the true Christian is not we never fall, but if we fall we have Jesus Christ to help us get back up. Many Heavy Weight Boxing champions have been knocked down, only to return in the later rounds to win. So it is with us; we may be down at times but we get back up before the bell rings and the fight is over.

Inner Healing takes place when we pour out our heart to God; we empty ourselves of our own plans, hopes, ambitions, pride and self-sufficiency and ask God to search our entire heart, the deepest recesses and territory within the Undiscovered Country, to bind up our broken heart and comfort our morning, and provide the oil of gladness, a garment of praise instead of the spirit of discouragement and despair; to drive out the enemy and set fire to his camp---the fire of the Holy Ghost---and set us at liberty, who have been bruised.

The healing of past hurts and bruised emotions will effect a lasting change in the way we think. The renewing of the mind and the balancing of the intellect, emotions, will and imagination will also happen; the removal of unclean spirits, strongholds, delusions, vain imaginations, thinking distortions and the territorial spirit control that we believed as truth will be revealed for what they are----lies!

Before we know it, the mind will quiet and have less background chatter going on (demons are gone, no more board meetings). And we will be able to sleep soundly, awaken refreshed, and have a closer, intimate relationship with God.

To Know Christ: The word "know" in biblical sense means a lot more than a casual acquaintance or intellectual knowledge of someone or something.

To know, for example in Adam's or Abraham's case, meant to have sexual relations with, to also be legally married to that person; apart from the biblical use of "laid with," which implies sexual union without the benefits of marriage, and thus the Blessing of God that accompanies holy matrimony isn't present; the latter is sin and a negative soul-tie.

Therefore to know Christ is more than going to Church, preaching, teaching, singing, ushering, board membership, tithing and all the other important functions that make up the local churches; but knowing Christ apart from services, programs, duties and people.

We desire to have these open lines of communication but someone or something keeps getting in our way. We feel the power of His Presence while the praise and worship music is playing, during the preaching and prayer line, but as soon as we leave, it's as though God lives in the brick and mortar building but not in us; or, the Anointing stays with us for a while then fades like the perfume or cologne we strategically applied at 8:00 a.m. in the morning but now it's 10:00 p.m. and dark outside.

Fading glory isn't what God desires for us; ever-increased glory is what He wants; and we will have what we say. The reason that we experience the tremendous power of God while in the Church building is the Corporate Anointing.

Jesus said that where two or three are gathered together in His Name that He would be in the midst of them. It is equally true that an intercessory-prayer-strengthened Corporate Anointing blocks out the overhead local demonic powers that interfere in our lives via mental oppression, suggestions and phobias.

Another reason why we cannot experience Christ in us is the presence of demonic spirits in our soul or physical body; these evil entities may be silenced, made ineffective while we're in the Presence of Christ and His Anointing, but revive and function when we leave the Church and His Corporate Presence.

Religious spirits of tradition, legalism or formalism could be present but silenced during the service; they are spirits that deceive us to believe that Sunday morning Church is good, in that it also makes us look and feel good about ourselves; it's all that's needed for spiritual maturity, and all that God requires of us as devote Christians. So the rest of the week is ours, unless we decide to attend an optional Bible Study and Prayer meeting.

But, then again, we can't blame Satan for everything. Still another reason is that our flesh isn't under the complete control of our human spirit who is indwelled and being led by the Holy Spirit; there's a part that's still "us", and not conformed to the image of Jesus Christ. What percentage of Christ verses us---90-10, 70-30, 50-50, 20-80 etc., decides who's in control of our life.

The lower the percentage of Christ-control in us, the easier it is to return to our old self-life and our scandalous ways. As Christians we received the Holy Spirit as a complete Person: 100%. We didn't receive a "part" or "piece" of Him; but we do have control over how much He effects change in us. In general, sin has attached to it a pleasure principle; if sin always brought excruciating pain every time, no one but the most hard core sadist would have anything to do with it.

Because sin is pleasurable, the body and mind remembers it well, and tried to return to it every chance it gets. If the mind of the flesh (or lust of the flesh), as the Word describes this principle, reasons on a non-spiritual (assisted by Christ) but religious level that to be a good Christian it is wrong to participate in certain sin, it will counter-reason and subconsciously seek another outlet to express its desires.

For example: you may stop drinking alcohol and have years of "clean time" and you did it because it's the Christian thing to do, but now you occasionally visit a phonographic website to view naked women/men; or a chat line to talk to single women when we are married and our wife is asleep in the bedroom, then we have only exchanged one sin for another, and not been set free. Nevertheless, if we are determined to know Christ in us, there is a lot to overcome in this world.

God told Jeremiah and it also applies to us: "Call upon Me, and I will answer you" (Jer. 33:3). In this century of technology: Satellites, Internet, social networks, electronics, Voice Mail and E-Mail, it's relatively easy to contact people providing they want to be contacted! But none of it will help us contact God.

This is because God communicates at a different level, and has different means of communication. He often uses the "inner" channel; it's His private line. Not only can God communicate, but He has promised in His Word to answer us if we by faith call upon the Name of Jesus. This alone expresses His will towards us: He is able and willing to help! He said, "Ask, and you shall receive, that your joy may be full" (Jn. 16:24).

What we confess with our mouth is also important to what our experience in Christ becomes. The Word in Romans 10:9 says, "If you will confess with your mouth the Lord Jesus, and believe in your heart that God raised Him from the dead, you will be saved."

In the same way that faith is important to receive Salvation, faith is equally important to receive physical healing or spiritual deliverance from the oppression of indwelling evil spirits. A vocal confession establishes in the earth what is believed [adhered to, trusted in and relied on] in the heart. There are two biblical

Confessions: The Confession of sin and the Confession of Faith; both are needed in the entire Christian journey.

After Salvation, the Confession of sin only applies when we sin after accepting Jesus as Savior and Lord (Jn.3:16). But the Confession of Faith is needed to receive from God what's needed in our life and the lives of others; this includes Deliverance. It is necessary to pray and speak the Word of God to specifically target indwelling or familiar spirits in our life. Jesus sent His Word to deliver us from bondage; it is for freedom that Christ has set us free.

Let's look at Joshua and how he obtained the Promise: "Every place where your foot shall step, I have given it to you for an inheritance" (Josh. 1:3). This word of promise was given to Joshua and the Children of Israel to stir up their dormant faith in the God, Jehovah--whom the majority of the Israelites didn't know, because they were too young to remember the former attempt by their parents.

Their parents, because of their unbelief and a lack of faith, failed to obtain their inheritance. God was telling this group that faith is a  possessor of the promises of God, that  they should focus their minds and hearts upon  Him who is their Source — for the battle isn't theirs but the Lord's. God encouraged them;

He motivated them to believe His words as though the Promised Land was already theirs----which spiritually (by faith) it already was! They were raised up for such a time as this to be conquerors, to take by the force of faith the Promise that God made.

Even today, we as Christians are to by Faith, take possession of the promises of God that have been written in the Word of God and purchased by the Blood of Jesus Christ. We are to press in and take by  the Spirit what the Word of God generously states belongs to us; by the violence of the Holy Spirit, we are to by faith take our healing, deliverance, peace, joy, finances, etc., from the clutches and stranglehold of the devil!

We drive out the Anakims of unbelief and fear---spirits who have come between us and our covenant rights. And we do not stop until our life and our love ones are completely taken over-taken by the blessings of God by Jesus Christ."For we wrestle not against flesh and blood, but against principalities, against powers, against the rulers of the darkness of this world, against spiritual wickedness in the high places" (Eph. 6:12).

Does every Believer in Jesus Christ need Inner Healing? The answer to that question is Yes! As the above scripture indicates, there is a controlling demonic government reigning and ruling over the residents of the physical world. The descendents of Adam and Eve who are born into this world are under the curse of the Mosaic Law (except Jesus of Nazareth, the Christ).

We are born in sin, spiritually dead, and therefore subject to the ruler of this world---Satan. Everyone, Christian or non- Christian are exposed to the control-ling and manipulative influence of these principalities, powers, rulers, and high-seated personalities on a daily basis.

These demonic spirits began influencing and forming our thought patterns, by way of activating generational curses, creating mental and physical strongholds and bondages before we are born; in the womb spirits of rejection and fear are often imparted by way of the parent's attitude towards the unborn child.

Even the best of parents are only human, and subject to impart by way of oral instruction, discipline, lifestyle, or association, the wisdom accumulated in and of this world which is demonic and self destructive.  It is certain that the worst of parents will impose his or her beliefs, attitudes, prejudices, habits or worldly standards on their children. Associations and soul ties at school, work, fiats, lodges, fornication, media, music lyrics and people with toxic personalities add to the need to receive Jesus Christ's His Inner Healing and Deliverance.

When we accept Jesus Christ as our personal Lord and Savior, the Holy Spirit indwells our human spirit and causes us to be spiritually alive. The presence of the Holy Spirit establishes ownership, and thus the process of Sanctification commences: We are set apart to serve God; it also includes Inner Healing and Deliverance, to conforms us into the image of Jesus Christ by the renewing of the mind, healing of emotional trauma, instruction in the Word of God—thus countering the lie, the breaking of curses and the ejecting of demonic spirits.

Inner Healing and Deliverance is necessary because we also have a soul body (intellect, emotions, and will) and a physical body also. Within these two parts of the whole (spirit body, soul body, physical body), the need to uncover and address the hidden root causes of infirmity are necessary.

This is accomplished by dealing with the mental processes, behaviors, practices, curses, soul ties, emotions, disobedience, parental relationship, sexual sin, strongholds, bondages, addictions and places of frequent visitation have to be addressed and reconciled by way of the cross of Jesus Christ.

These things must suffer death, so that the life of Christ and the effectual power of His resurrected life and the truth will have His way not only where He dwells in the spirit body, but also in the soul and physical body. Then He can bring healing and deliverance to the entire person; and use that person to touch the lives of others in the Body of Christ and the world.

As Sanctification is a lifelong process, so is Inner healing and Deliverance. Because the average Christian has experienced many years of "world programming," it doesn't suddenly disappear in a few hours of an Inner Healing and Deliverance session. In the same manner that we are instructed to work out our own salvation, we are to do the same in our getting set free from the contamination of the world.

Notes

# Chapter Five

### Inner Healing and Deliverance

27 "And it shall come to pass in that day, that his [Satan's] burden shall be taken away from off thy shoulders, and his yoke from off thy [our] neck, and the yoke shall be destroyed because of the anointing. 19 When the enemy [Satan] shall come in, like a flood the spirit of the lord shall lift up a standard against him" Isa. 10.27; 59.19 (KJV).

Adam was entrusted with the Word of God. The Word of God was every word that proceeded out of His mouth. Among these words were commands that Adam "be fruitful and multiply and replenish the earth, and subdue it; and have dominion..." (Genesis 1:28).

Thus because of the Word of God, Adam reigned as god of this world. Since it was the results of God's Word that Adam was given dominion and authority, it was also the disobeying of God's Word that ultimately caused Adam to lose his dominion and authority. The modus operandi of the Word hasn't changed.

Therefore, it's OUR FAITH in God's Word that maintains an activation of His Word in our lives. The FAITH OF GOD is inherited in His Word. Our faith must unite with the Faith inherited in the Word to bring it to pass in our lives. In short, we must AGREE WITH THE WORD OF GOD.

18 "[For Abraham, human reason for] hope being gone, hoped IN FAITH that he should become the father of many nations, as he

had been PROMISED, So [numberless] shall your descendants be"--- Ro. 4.18-21 (Amp. Bible).

"Human reason" often defies and defiles our Faith in the Word of God. The life of Abraham was not a life without temptations and controversy. His story wasn't recorded in the Holy Bible because he was perfect, a faultless example, or even that he fathered a child when he was "as good as dead" because of his age.

Abraham wasn't known for the fact that Sarah's womb was barren, and the miracle that God performed in restoring her womb; and her natural beauty was such that King Abimelech---whom could have had his pick of the younger women---was dazzled and wanted her, though she was actually a senior citizen!

And though Abraham was twice struck down by a spirit of fear concerning his personal safety when traveling with Sarah, and he lied to King Abimelech, Abraham was known for his faith in God. Abraham, for the most part, believed that God was able to keep His promises. He considered not his natural ability, his physical appearance, wealth, community ties or what other people believed, but considered Him who would do exceeding and abundantly above all he could ask or think.

"Abraham believed God and it was counted unto him for righteousness" (Romans 4:3). Abraham believed in Him who justifies the ungodly (Romans 4:5). Abraham wasn't perfect but served a perfect God, who justified him by his faith, not works, and counted his faith as righteousness (Romans 4:22).

"Therefore being justified by faith, we have PEACE WITH GOD through our Lord Jesus Christ" (Romans 4:25). The peace we enjoy was purchased at the cross. Salvation, Sanctification, Healing and Deliverance was purchased by the Blood of Jesus Christ. It's by faith that we appropriate the dominion Christ won for us.

As only by faith Adam, Abraham, the prophets and *Jesus* could please God, the Way has not changed. The Spiritual Laws do not apply to some people and not others. "But without faith it is IMPOSSIBLE TO PLEASE HIM; for he that cometh to God must BELIEVE that He is, and that He is a rewarder of them that DILIGENTLY seek Him" (Hebrews 11:6). We must first believe in the promises of God and that He will keep His promises. These are the two immutable concepts: God has made promises and God cannot lie.

The yoke-destroying power of the Anointing will drive out the Enemy. Like a flood, the Spirit of the Lord will lift up the heavenly standard of righteousness and bring about peace, healings and deliverances from the torments of demonic oppressions. His promises are available to whosoever will ask in Jesus' Name.

When the Enemy comes in he comes to stay. It's not a visit but an occupation; it's not to steal our television, jewelry or sports car--but our health, soul and spirit. He came to steal, kill and destroy everything of eternal weight in glory. The peace and tranquility of undisturbed rest and love is his target.

"He **deliverer** and **rescues,** and works signs and wonders in the heaven and in the earth, who hath delivered Daniel from the power of the lions" (Daniel 6:27). Daniel was delivered from the bone-crushing jaws of the hungry lions. His destruction was imminent; the plan was presumed flawless. But the Enemy didn't take into account Daniel's faith in God.

He was a man who knew the worth of prayer. Daniels faith transcended the physical realm and threat of danger, and delivered him from the power of the evil spirits using the satraps who got Daniel into the lion's den.

The schemes of the ruling spirits manipulated King Darius and his satraps. But God delivered Daniel from the obvious danger and the invisible attack. In fact, it was King Darius who praised God for Daniel's miraculous deliverance! The king realized the error of his ways--how he allowed people and his gods (who were actually evil spirits pretending to be God) manipulate him into doing evil. He came to believe in Daniel's God. He proclaimed in faith: "He **delivers** and **rescues**". The Enemy came in but was swept away by the life-changing flood of the Spirit of God.

The Prophet Joel wrote: "And it shall come to pass, that whosoever shall call upon the name of the Lord shall be **delivered** (Joel 2:32). while the apostle Paul wrote: "for whosoever shall call upon the name of the lord shall be **saved**" (Romans 10:13).

We discover that Deliverance was available before Salvation was; yet Salvation, the New Birth includes the provisions of Deliverance; and yet both are the Ministry of the Holy Spirit. In Christ we deal with Satan in a different way than the Old Testament.

Jesus proclaimed in the synagogue, "The Spirit of the Lord is upon Me, because He hath **anointed me** to preach the gospel to the poor; He bath sent Me to heal the brokenhearted, to preach **deliverance** to the captives, and recovering of sight to the blind, to set at liberty them that are bruised, to preach the acceptable year of the lord" (Lk. 4.18,19).

It was the Spirit of the Lord, the Holy Spirit that was upon the man named Jesus of Nazareth. That Spirit, the Anointing empowered Jesus to preach and do the Father's will. The Christ within Jesus, the Kingdom of God, cast out and eradicated everything contrary to His nature; bondages, sicknesses, diseases/ poverty and death were challenged by Jesus and He claimed the victory over them. It was not who He was as a human being that made the difference. Certainly, it was the Anointing that brought the victory, the Presence of the Kingdom of God upon the scene.

"When the evening was come, they brought unto Him many that were possessed with devils: and he cast out the spirits with His word, and healed all that were sick: That it might be fulfilled which was spoken by Esaias (Isaiah) the prophet, saying, **Himself took our infirmities, and bare our sicknesses**" (Mt. 8.16, 17).

The scriptures point out that the deliverance work of the Lord was foretold centuries earlier. He fulfilled the will of God by Himself taking our infirmities, sicknesses and diseases. Yet that wasn't the end of the prophesies: "Himself" doesn't only mean Jesus of Nazareth ministering on earth for three years, but ministering FOREVER as the Christ, the Son of God.

Therefore, when the Anointing is upon us it's the Lord Jesus Christ ministering--Himself casting out sicknesses and diseases. Because the Anointing is Christ, we cannot accept any credit for the miracles performed through us. We humble ourselves and strive to become obedient unto death as was Jesus. As Abraham had no confidence in the flesh neither do we.

"And when He had called unto Him His twelve disciples, He gave them POWER AGAINST UNCLEAN SPIRITS, TO CAST THEM OUT, AND TO HEAL ALL MANNER OF SICKNESS AND ALL MANNER OF DISEASES" (Matthew 10:1). This was still HIMSELF working in the earth. The disciples were only His instruments. The power they received was the Holy Spirit; it was delegated authority to minister under the same covenant Jesus ministered under.

God cannot and will not interfere in our lives without our permission; and God has done all He's going to do concerning these spirits--He triumphed over them by the cross. "That through death [and the resurrection that followed] He might destroy him that had the power over death, that is, the Devil" (Hebrews 2:14). He abolished the Devil's authority over the children of God (the unsaved are still in the Devil's family.), and the sting of death. He gave the Church authority to heal and cast out demons. What a remarkable Lord!

The Prayer of Agreement was another secret that Jesus revealed. "If two of you shall agree..." will manifest the Third, HIMSELF, bringing to bear the corporate Anointing that is upon the entire Church.

### The Armor Of God

10 "...be strong in the Lord and the power of His might. 11 Put on the whole armor of God, that ye may be able to stand against the wiles of the Devil. 14...girt about with Truth...Breastplate of Righteousness 15...feet Shod with the Preparation of the Gospel of Peace. 16...Shield of Faith.17...Helmet of Salvation, and the Sword of the Spirit, which is the Word of God" Eph. 6.10,11,14-17.

Though we're seated In Him, in the Third Heaven, and at the Throne of God, our Soul and Physical Bodies live within the realms of demonic activity; our self-life and consciousness is an assignment for demon spirits. When we were Born Again and positioned with Christ, we were granted access to the body armor of the saints of God. We can--and must--put on the armor of God and then stand against the schemes of the unclean devils on the ground and in the atmosphere around us.

The **Belt of Truth** fights the lies and deceptions of Satan. He wants us to think that he has more authority than Jehovah-Elohim or Christians. Satan wants us to believe that he maintains complete control of the world, and the destinies of the 6.7 billion people who live on Earth. Only the Word of God, the Truth can make us free.

The **Breastplate of Righteousness** is God's approval, His Justifying us by Faith in Jesus Christ, the Messiah. Satan attacks our mind, our emotions and tells us we'll always be sinners--snarling pitiful creatures. But the Word states that we're the righteousness of God

In Christ Jesus. God loves and approves of us; God sees us as the Children of the Resurrection. We're In Him and He's in us. We are loved, accepted and blessed with all spiritual blessings.

The **Shoes** represent our being prepared by the Holy Spirit to be used in His Ministry; it's our submission to the Divine Purpose, our willingness to do good works, to produce good fruit, that Jehovah-Elohim will receive glory. We're saved by Grace through Faith--yet to advance and buildup the Kingdom of God on Earth we witness, testify, teach and preach the Word of Faith. We minister through Agape Love, Healing and Deliverance to all peoples, across denominations, racial and economic lines.

The Anointing on the feet, and the armor of the Shoes quenches the fiery darts of Satan who wants us to believe that witnessing to the lost is a waste of time and money.

Satan whispers that there are too many countries, people, languages and dialects to successfully reach the 6.7 Billion people; he says that there are insurmountable racial, cultural, political and religious barriers--obstacles he has placed there--and not enough committed workers, financial resources to purchase food, medicine and personal needs to reach the hardest hit areas on the planet.

But Satan is a liar! The Anointing on the feet and the armor of the Shoes defeats Satan.

The **Shield of Faith** protects us from demonic attacks through the invisible realm against our mind and body. The Shield of Faith protects us from mental, emotional and physical attacks, insults, temptations and hindrances to our prayer and Calling.

We believe, have Faith in the Word of God, trust in and rely on God's promises. We therefore enforce the New Testament Covenant with zeal, an available and humble spirit of devotion. Often the Spiritual Gift of Faith, the Faith of God manifests as He adds to our faith, His Faith, to reinforce our shielding during the heaviest of satanic attacks. The command to <u>stand</u> resides in us. The **Helmet of Salvation**: Salvation is the area of Satan's first strike. If he failed to stop us from getting Saved, his next move is to persuade us to doubt our Salvation, or to enter into the trap of unbelief concerning the Word of God.

Satan wants us to doubt the greatness of Jesus Christ, His Name, His Blood and His victory at Calvary. Satan wants us to doubt God's ability to keep His promises and perform His Word as written in the Holy Bible. Satan wants us to doubt our position In Him and at His Throne in the Third Heaven; to believe that the promises and Anointing of God was only for the Jewish prophets and leaders of ancient Israel, the Old Testament days and the early church history.

Satan wants to rob us of the Blessing. He doesn't want us to experience the Faith and joy of our Salvation. But the Anointing of God, the Helmet of Salvation bulldozes through the dung heap of Satan's crappy schemes; Satan has no wind to run this race with us! The **Sword of the Spirit** is the Word of God. Jesus said, "It is written..." The Word of God rising from our heart and spoken out of our mouth sends Satan and his troops fleeing for parts unknown.

We being rooted and grounded in the Word provides us with a mammoth-size sword to strike down the oppression, obsession, depression and possession by unclean spirits. We pray and stand our ground, waiting patiently for the Word of God to manifest, the Sword of the Spirit to fall. If doubt or any such deception comes we slice it with our Sword.

We can't afford to let the Word of God depart from before our eyes, for He has magnified His Word above all His Name. We as doers of the Word and not hears only overcome the world.

## Spiritual Warfare

"The weapons we fight with are not <u>weapons</u> of the <u>world.</u> ...they have <u>divine power</u> to <u>demolish strongholds"</u> 2 Cor. 10:4 (NIV).

The strongholds that Paul wrote about aren't the Second Heaven Demonic Government; we're not to be overly concerned but aware of its existence and influence. The strongholds we're concerned with exist in our mind. The thoughts, feelings, emotions and imaginations--the desires of the flesh, eyes, and the pride of the self-life and conformity to the world system--are the strongholds to be taken captive and brought down by obedience to the Word of God.

"And be not conformed to this world: but be ye **transformed** by the **renewing of your mind**..." (Ro. 12:2). Face it, we have issues to work on. These issues are predominately from the past, brought into the present by our mental functions of memory and emotions; or tormenting spirits use our negative history in the present to manipulate, intimidate and dominate us, through our thought-stream; these thoughts and feelings have a powerful effect on our present thoughts and behaviors.

These strongholds, attitudes, prejudices, codes, beliefs that we've lived by as an un-regenerated sinner, are presently affecting our relationship with Jesus and His Body. Nevertheless, through the unsearchable riches of Jesus Christ, has He conferred upon His heirs an arsenal of spiritual weaponry.

These weapon systems intercept and cancel the works of Satan and the works **of** the flesh. We wield the nine **Fruit of the Spirit** to assist us: **Love, Joy, Peace, Patience, Kindness, Goodness, Faithfulness, Meekness and Self-Control** (Gal. 5.22,23).

The second order of spiritual weapons, the **Spiritual Gifts** are: **Tongues, Interpretation of Tongues, Gifts of Healing, Prophecy, Word of Wisdom, Word of Knowledge, Discerning of Spirits, Faith and Working of Miracles** (1 Cor. 12.8-11). These gifts also detect and monitor the demonic activity around us. From our position in the Third Heaven we can know in advance what Satan has planned, even his "local" maneuvers and operations.

Through the Spiritual Gifts we crush Satan's resistance to the New Testament Covenant, his attacks upon us in defiance to God's authority, and who we are In Christ. Together these eighteen weapons and "radar" systems help us get the victory over our mind, the world, and the evil spirits.

Jesus Christ gave us government within His Body that occupies the Earth; the field offices are the Five-Fold Ministry: Apostles, Prophets, Evangelists, Pastors, Teachers (Eph. 4:11). We Believers receive instructions through our official leaders. Jesus Christ is our Commander-in-Chief; these leaders are likened to generals. None of the weapons of our warfare are conventional, nuclear, biological or chemical--but they can utterly loose the bonds of wickedness and undue every yoke!

The "It is written..." attitude in prayer and speech must replace the old unprofitable "begging" God to do what He has already empowered us to do by Faith; or seeking Deliverance from demons, when the problem is that we're too lazy to study, believe and practice the Word of God, thus our mind isn't significantly renewed. The flesh can't be exorcised--cast off the bone; only demon spirits can be cast out.

19 "The acts of the sinful nature (the works of the flesh) are obvious: sexual immorality, impurity and debauchery, 20 idolatry and witchcraft; hatred, discord, jealousy, fits of rage, selfish ambition, dissensions, factions, 21 and envy; drunkenness, orgies, and the like"--- Galatians 5.19-21 (NIV).

The inference of this scripture is upon **we** as a Christian to crucify the fleshly desires, not storming the demonic realms or praying down the Spiritual Wickedness in the heavens--but accepting responsibility, accountability and obtaining control of our mental thoughts, emotions, feelings and actions.

We have to **work out our own Salvation**, renewing of our mind, as a partner with the Holy Spirit. He isn't going to do all the work and we can't do it without Him. We don't want to indulge, go back to the old sinful "works of the flesh", so we have to be diligent. Relaxing and meditating on the Word can break the compulsive, neurotic or psychotic merry-go-round of repetitive sinful habits that you can't conquer by sheer will power.

The Word has Deliverance and Healing power. "He sent His Word and healed them" (Ps. 107:20). Hindrance to our spiritual growth is our old ways standing in the way of our new ways. Unbelief and doubt opposes Faith.

### Inner Healing and Deliverance

Luke 6:46 Jesus said, "Why do you call Me, Lord, Lord, and do not what I say?" There are a number of reasons why we do not obey the Lord as we desire to. Many of these reasons point to the need for Inner Healing and Deliverance.

The character of our New Man, recreated in Christ Jesus, is being defiled by the "bitter root" character of our Old Man; the nature of our Old Man, as described in Hebrews 12:15, has not been fully taken to the cross of Christ to experience death, and is clandestinely plotting to overthrow the Lordship of Jesus Christ over us, Whose Holy Spirit resides in our human spirits. The Old Sin Nature desires to express itself through our self-life by sprouting roots of influence, in order to reclaim its leadership position.

## Evangelizing Unbelieving Hearts

Hebrews 3:12 "take care, **brethren** (the church) lest there be in any one of you an evil, unbelieving heart, in falling away from the living God." Because the Old Man refuses to remain dead, deep in our hearts there remains some measure of unbelief. Inner Healing is actually evangelism, a ministry bringing the Gospel to those parts of a Believer's heart that have not yet believed and received Salvation. Romans 10:9 states that it is "belief in the heart" that brings salvation: Much of what we have acquired of the Gospel is divided between "heart belief" and "head knowledge". Many Christians cannot live the Gospel because they have believed only with the mind; their faith has not totally conquered their hearts.

The Ministry of Inner Healing is to reach the hearts of born-again Christians with the good news of salvation. V.10 "For with the heart man believes, resulting in righteousness, and with the mouth he confesses, resulting in. salvation." So, the Ministry of Inner Healing is to evangelize the unbelieving hearts of believers; it is the application of the blood and cross and resurrection life of our Lord Jesus Christ to those stubborn dimensions of believer's hearts (including character flaws, strongholds, bondages and personality disorders) that have so far refused the redemption their minds and spirits requested when they invited Jesus in. Often this refusal is the presence or influence of unclean spirits in the soul or physical bodies.

## Inner Healing and Sanctification

Salvation or Regeneration comes after we have repented, confessed our sins and by faith accepted Jesus Christ as our Lord and Savior, then we miraculously receive the indwelling of the Holy Spirit in our human spirits, which raises us from spiritual death to spiritual life. After that comes Sanctification, which is the lifelong process in which the Holy Spirit transforms our mind (Romans 12:2), character and personality to be exactly like Jesus. The Ministry of Inner Healing is a tool of the Holy Spirit to effect changes in our individual lives. Inner Healing does not erase a memory or change our personal history. Rather it enables us to cherish even the worst moments in our lives, for through them God has inscribed eternal lessons onto our hearts and prepared us to minister to all who have suffered in the same way. In this, Romans 8:28 is clear; All things do work together for the good to those who love God and are called according to His purpose.

### What is Inner Healing?

Inner healing is the healing of memories and emotions, the taking to the cross of Christ the self, that it may experience death, the application of the crucified and resurrected Life of Jesus Christ; it is also prayer, biblical counseling to effect mental and spiritual stability, Sanctification, consecration which leads to Transformation.

The difference between Psychology and Inner Healing is that Inner Healing is based on the Word of God; the Christian is to die to the self life, self will, self oriented goals and motivations that are outside of God's will and purpose for his life.

Psychology seeks to restore a person's self-image, an image given to him by the world system of standards; this philosophy is based on the theory that if the person sees himself in a good light, he will have the confidence to perform well: it is like creating a sinner who thinks well of himself, a new and improved sinner.

### Six steps to Inner Healing & Deliverance:
(6 is the number of Man.)

1. Renunciation
2. Forgiveness

3. Humility
4. Prayer
5. Repentance
6. Warfare

## Four Levels of demonic activity in humans.

**First Level** Infestation: Demonic spirit have gathered about a person but not inside of him. Example: Blocking Spirits and Familiar Spirits.

**Second Level:** Inhabitation: Demonic spirit has entered but has been limited by the Holy Spirit.

**Third Level:** Obsession: Inhabiting Demon has come out of hiding to assume control of character structure. In Un-believers and Nominal Christians demon can live within the inmost self and control psychologically Spirit-Filled Christians, through negative or sinful emotions, hidden motives and attitudes in the members.

**Fourth Level:** Possession or Owner-ship, original personality entirely suppressed. Christians cannot be possessed.

## Spiritual Principles

1.    Demons cannot read our mind.
2.    Demons attack Saved and Unsaved people.
3.    Inner Healing isn't confessing old sins.
4.    Everything bad that happens to us isn't demonic.
5.    Demons  must be  invited in before they can occupy a Christian.
6.    All Christians have the authority to cast out demons.
7.    Demons can attack through another person.
8.    Demons can talk through the mouth of people.

9.   Demons can communicate thoughts  and ideas or  talk to the mind of a  person without the person being  conscious or aware of it.
10.  Deliverance Ministers are protected by the Holy Spirit from demons attempting to transfer from client to them.
11.  Deliverance is exorcism, the casting out of demons.
12.  Sickness and Disease is often but not always attributed  to demons in the soul (mind/concious)  or physical bodies.

Adamic Sin, Generational Sin, Curses, Disobedience and sinful lifestyle gives demons a legal right to torment and inhabit. Demons are fallen angels and cannot be Saved. Satan is the prince of the demonic kingdom.

## Laying On of Hands

17 "And these signs shall follow them that believe: In My Name they shall cast out devils...18 ...they shall lay hands on the sick, and they shall recover"---Mk. 16.17,18 (KJV).

The Doctrine of the Laying on of Hands has become a controversial topic in the latter day reign of the Church. According to Jesus, the Apostles and the Believers of the early Church, the Laying on of Hands was a part of the exercise of faith in  the Lord Jesus, and there were plenty of miracles.

Jesus commanded (not suggested) "all" His disciples to cast out devils and lay hands on the sick, as demonstrating the delegated authority that He gave us. He also said that certain signs shall follow the Believer. The ordinations, presbyteries, missionary journeys and healing services were energized by the Laying on of Hands.

The "fear merchants"---those who quickly point out a dreadful consequence to a true scriptural action---in order to satisfy their carnal or religious beliefs, interpret as doctrines their own opinions as holy scripture. The merchants make logical arguments and excuses to condone their failure to obey the Lord's Commandment regarding exorcising demons and healing the sick.

So today the traditional, denominational pastors just want to preach to a well-dressed audience, pick up their check and go home. To justify their religious doctrines, with Satan's guidance, thousands of pastors shout "BEWARE" OF SATAN!" to their Church members who want to obey Jesus by laying hands on demonized or diseased persons; they are cautioned that demons or sick- nesses would transfer to the Christian or their family.

They quote 1 Timothy 5:22 which states, "Lay hands on no man suddenly," which isn't a reference to demons or sickness, but Paul was advising Timothy against appointing Church leaders who were new Christians, whose character was questionable or not known. Hands were laid on Church leaders when they were installed in office!

Today many Church leaders misuse the above scripture and in so doing imply that Satan has more powerful than God; then young Christians wonder why so many pastors leave their pulpits of because gross sin was discovered in their lives. These pastors needed Deliverance but were too proud to ask for help. Many Church leaders stand behind their "safe" philosophy when dealing with something they know little or nothing about: Deliverance.

They lack information and the determined purpose to seek out the whole truth; they lack faith to believe in the progressive work of the Holy Spirit, called Sanctification. To them, everything stopped at the cross, a finished work. Then, why is there so much sinning in the Body of Christ? How is it that we need a crowbar to pry a Christian's hand off the arm of a slot machine? Or worst, from around someone's neck!

Pastors who lack adequate faith in Deliverance and Healing teach the congregation of the dreadful consequences in stepping out of the boat; they always tell the story of how Peter's lack of faith caused him to sink, but not the fact that he got out the boat, walked on the water, while the other eleven watched safely from the boat; at least Peter got out the boat! He did his best to obey Jesus who said to him, "Come."

Old wives tales, worn-out traditions and scare tactics---all of which are satanic in origin, has made the Word of God of no effect in the lives of many Christians. They cannot get victory over sickness, disease or demons because they are afraid to let another Christian lay hands on them!

Know that by faith we are protected by the Spirit of God to receive help and to give our help; we are protected by the Blood of Jesus, and cannot be "compromised" by unclean spirits while in the performance of our Christian duties. The spirit of fear is the reason why a lot of us are without spiritual strength, or having great difficulty in fulfilling our destinies.

But hold on. help is on the way. We must say out loud: It is for freedom that Christ has set me free!

Let us not be like King Saul, who in his last days came to this conclusion: "I have played the fool, and have erred exceedingly!"--- 1 Sam. 26.21.

It is for freedom that Christ has set us free. Let's enjoy it.

# Chapter Five

## Domestic Violence

One dimension of Spiritual Warfare is to combat and slow down the progression, proliferation and expansion of evil on the earth. This is done through the intercessions and prayers of devote Believers in Jesus Christ, standing on the Word of God, and wielding the Sword of the Spirit, the Word of God.

Violence come in many forms. Here are a few examples: There are violent military actions, maneuvers and operations taking place at any given time all over the world; there is criminal violence, terrorism, serial killers, murderers, robbers, assaults rapists, gang and street violence. Most of these forms of violence take place outside of the home, though many fall victim to Home Invasion violence.

The Prince Spirits that govern geographical areas and territories precipitate different types of violence. These high level demons use the age-old divide and conquer from within strategy most effectively against Christians and non-Christians alike.

At the heart of the nation is its family life; at the heart of a household is also the family unit. If the Prince Spirits can destroy the bond between two married people, then they can control that household, and eventually the nation. As this also applies to non-traditional or unmarried persons living together in relationships and cohabitations that are not recognized by God or the Church.

Domestic Violence is at world epidemic proportion. This evil phenomenon exist in every country around the globe; it is described and comes packaged in many shapes, form and fashions; but Love has nothing to do with it.

**Domestic violence**, also known as **Domestic Abuse, Spousal Abuse, Battering, Family Violence**, and **Intimate Partner Violence (IPV), Intimate Terrorism (IT),** is broadly defined as a pattern of abusive behaviors by one or both partners in an intimate relationship such as marriage, dating, family, or cohabitation. Domestic Violence, so defined, has many forms, including physical aggression (hitting, kicking, biting, shoving, restraining, slapping, throwing objects), or threats thereof; sexual abuse; emotional abuse; controlling or domineering; intimidation; stalking; passive/covert abuse (e.g., neglect); and economic deprivation.

The U. S. Office on Violence Against Women (OVW) defines Domestic Violence as a "pattern of abusive behavior in any relationship that is used by one partner to gain or maintain power and control over another intimate partner". The definition adds that domestic violence "can happen to anyone regardless of race, age, sexual orientation, religion, or gender", and can take many forms, including physical abuse, sexual abuse, emotional, economic, and psychological abuse.

All forms of Domestic Abuse have one purpose: to *gain and maintain control* over the victim. Abusers use many tactics to exert power over their spouse or partner: dominance, humiliation, isolation, threats, intimidation, denial and blame.

Another type is **Situational Couple Violence**, which arises out of conflicts that escalate to arguments and then to violence. It is not connected to a general pattern of control. Although it occurs less frequently in relationships and is less serious than Intimate Terrorism, in some cases it can be frequent and/or quite serious, even life-threatening. This is probably the most common type of Intimate Partner Violence.

The U.S. Centers for Disease Control, divide Domestic Violence into two types: Reciprocal Violence, in which both partners are violent, and Non-Reciprocal violence, in which one partner is violent.

## Sexual abuse

Sexual Abuse is any situation in which force or threat is used to obtain participation in unwanted sexual activity. Coercing a person to engage in sex, against their will, even if that person is a spouse or intimate partner with whom consensual sex has occurred, is an act of aggression and violence.

## Emotional abuse

Emotional Abuse (also called Psychological Abuse or Mental Abuse) can include humiliating the victim privately or publicly, controlling what the victim can and cannot do, withholding information from the victim, deliberately doing something to make the victim feel diminished or embarrassed, isolating the victim from friends and family, implicitly blackmailing the victim by harming others when the victim expresses independence or happiness, or denying the victim access to money or other basic resources and necessities.

Emotional Abuse can include Verbal Abuse and is defined as any behavior that threatens, intimidates, undermines the victim's self-worth or self-esteem, or controls the victim's freedom. This can include threatening the victim with injury or harm, telling the victim that they will be killed if they ever leave the relationship, and public humiliation.

Constant criticism, name-calling, and making statements that damage the victim's self-esteem are also common verbal forms of emotional abuse. Often perpetrators will use children to engage in emotional abuse by teaching them to harshly criticize the victim as well. Emotional Abuse includes conflicting actions or statements which are designed to confuse and create insecurity in the victim. These behaviors also lead the victim to question themselves, causing them to believe that they are making up the abuse or that the abuse is their fault.

Emotional Abuse includes forceful efforts to isolate the victim, keeping them from contacting friends or family. This is intended to eliminate those who might try to help the victim leave the relationship and to create a lack of resources for them to rely on if they were to leave. Isolation results in damaging the victim's sense of internal strength, leaving them feeling helpless and unable to escape from the situation.

People who are being emotionally abused often feel as if they do not own themselves; rather, they may feel that their significant other has nearly total control over them. Women or men under-going emotional abuse often suffer from depression, which puts them at increased risk for suicide, eating disorders, and drug and alcohol abuse.

**Verbal abuse** is a form of emotionally abusive behavior involving the use of language. It may include profanity but can occur with or without the use of expletives.

Verbal abuse may include aggressive actions such as name-calling, blaming, ridicule, disrespect, and criticism, but there are also less obviously aggressive forms of verbal abuse. Statements that may seem benign on the surface can be thinly veiled attempts to humiliate; falsely accuse; or manipulate others to submit to undesirable behavior; make others feel unwanted and unloved; threaten others economically; or isolate victims from support systems.

**Economic abuse** is a form of abuse when one intimate partner has control over the other partner's access to economic resources. Economic abuse may involve preventing a spouse from resource acquisition, limiting the amount of resources to use by the victim, or by exploiting economic resources of the victim.

The motive behind preventing a spouse from acquiring resources is to diminish victim's capacity to support him/herself, thus forcing him/her to depend on the perpetrator financially, which includes preventing the victim from obtaining education, finding employment, maintaining or advancing their careers, and acquiring assets. In addition, the abuser may also put the victim on an allowance, closely monitor how the victim spends money, spend victim's money without his/her consent and creating debt, or completely spend victim's savings to limit available resources.

3.3 million children witness domestic violence each year in the US. There has been an increase in acknowledgment that a child who is exposed to domestic abuse during their upbringing will suffer in their developmental and psychological welfare.

Due to the awareness of domestic violence that some children have to face, it also generally impacts how the child develops emotionally, socially, behaviorally as well as cognitively. Some emotional and behavioral problems that can result due to domestic violence include increased aggressiveness, anxiety, and changes in how a child socializes with friends, family, and authorities.

Depression, as well as self-esteem issues, can follow due to traumatic experiences. Problems with attitude and cognition in schools can start developing, along with a lack of skills such as problem-solving. Correlation has been found between the experience of abuse and neglect in childhood and perpetrating domestic violence and sexual abuse in adulthood.

Additionally, in some cases the abuser will purposely abuse the mother in front of the child to cause a ripple effect, hurting not one but two of his victims. It has been found that children who witness mother-assault are more likely to exhibit symptoms of posttraumatic stress disorder (PTSD).

### Physical

Bruises, broken bones, head injuries, lacerations, and internal bleeding are some of the acute effects of a domestic violence incident that require medical attention and hospitalization. Some chronic health conditions that have been linked to victims of domestic violence are arthritis, irritable bowel syndrome, chronic pain, pelvic pain, ulcers, and migraines. Victims who are pregnant during a domestic violence relationship experience greater risk of miscarriage, pre-term labor, and injury to or death of the fetus.

### Psychological

Among victims who are still living with their perpetrators, high amounts of stress, fear, and anxiety are commonly reported. Depression is also common, as victims are made to feel guilty for 'provoking' the abuse and are constantly subjected to intense criticism.

It is reported that 60% of victims meet the diagnostic criteria for depression, either during or after termination of the relationship, and have a greatly increased risk of suicidality. In addition to depression, victims of domestic violence also commonly experience long-term anxiety and panic, and are likely to meet the diagnostic criteria for Generalized Anxiety Disorder and Panic Disorder.

The most commonly referenced psychological effect of domestic violence is Post-Traumatic Stress Disorder (PTSD). PTSD (as experienced by victims) is characterized by flashbacks, intrusive images, exaggerated startle response, nightmares, and avoidance of triggers that are associated with the abuse. These symptoms are generally experienced for a long span of time after the victim has left the dangerous situation. Many researchers state that PTSD is possibly the best diagnosis for those suffering from psychological effects of domestic violence, as it accounts for the variety of symptoms commonly experienced by victims of trauma.

### Long-term

Domestic violence can trigger many different responses in victims, all of which are very relevant for any professional working with a victim. Major consequences of domestic violence victimization include psychological/mental health issues and chronic physical health problems. A victim's overwhelming lack of resources can lead to homelessness and poverty.

Many cases of domestic violence against women occur due to jealousy when the woman is either suspected of being unfaithful or is planning to leave the relationship.

The UN Declaration on the Elimination of Violence against Women (1993) states that "violence against women is a manifestation of historically unequal power relations between men and women, which has led to domination over and discrimination against women by men and to the prevention of the full advancement of women, and that violence against women is one of the crucial social mechanisms by which women are forced into a subordinate position compared with men."

Men kill their female intimate partners at about four times the rate that women kill their male intimate partners. Research by Jacquelyn Campbell, PhD RN FAAN has found that at least two thirds of women killed by their intimate partners were battered by those men prior to the murder. She also found that when males are killed by female intimates, the women in those relationships had been abused by their male partner about 75 percent of the time.

### The Scriptures

Both men and women were created in His image, as equal partners with distinctively different roles. Genesis 1:27.

Bible verses that give credence to patriarchy:

"Wives, submit to your own husbands, as to the Lord. For the husband is the head of the wife even as Christ is the head of the church, his body, and is himself its Savior. Now as the church submits to Christ, so also wives should submit in everything to their husbands" Ephesians 5:22-24.

According to the U.S. Conference of Catholic Bishops, "Men who abuse often use Ephesians 5:22, taken out of context, to justify their behavior, but the passage (v. 21-33) refers to the mutual submission of husband and wife out of love for Christ. Husbands should love their wives as they love their own body, as Christ loves the Church."

"Likewise, husbands, live with your wives in an understanding way, showing honor to the woman as the weaker vessel, since they are heirs with you of the grace of life, so that your prayers may not be hindered" 1 Peter 3:7.

"A woman should learn in quietness and full submission" 1 Timothy 2:11.

Verses that support discipline: "I do not permit a woman to teach or to have authority over a man; she must be silent" 1 Timothy 2:12.

"A woman should learn in quietness and full submission" (Separate or isolate) 1 Timothy 2:11.

The teachers of the law and the Pharisees brought in a woman caught in adultery. They made her stand before the group and said to Jesus, "Teacher, this woman was caught in the act of adultery. In the Law Moses commanded us to stone such women. Now what do you say?" John 8:3-5.

The husband has authority to discipline the wife. The wife does not have authority to discipline her husband. Genesis 3:16.

"Now no chastening for the present seems to be joyous, but grievous: nevertheless afterward it yields the peaceable fruit of righteousness unto them which are exercised thereby" Hebrews 12:11.

Bible verses are often used to justify domestic abuse, such as those that refer to male superiority and female submission, but use of violence is a misinterpreted view of the male role. For instance, Eve (Genesis 2-3), is often misinterpreted, particularly by Christians, to be disobedient to patriarchal God and man, and to many a generalized symbol of womanhood that must be submissive and subject to discipline.

There are some Christians who believe that it is the man's duty and right to discipline his wife, usually by spanking, such as the consensual Christian Domestic Discipline (CDD).

Verse that does not support beating:  "Husbands, love your wives, and do not be harsh with them. Colossians 3:19.

## Incidence of domestic violence among Christians

Christian women are often silent and accepting of any domestic violence that they may suffer. In the 1970s when programs were initiated to train church leaders about domestic violence, *But no one ever comes to me with this problem* was the most common response. Church leaders often believed that if no one was reaching out for assistance within the church that there was no problem in their church, however, women often withheld discussing their problems over concern that it would not be handled appropriately.

When women became pastors they found that much of their time became devoted to handling domestic abuse and other forms of violence against women; Their involvement included crisis intervention.

Among all Christians, 37.5% live in the Americas (11.4% in the United States), 25.7% live in Europe, 22.5% live in Africa, 13.1% live in Asia, 1.2% live in Oceania and 0.9% live in the Middle East.

The following information is for some of the countries with 92% and more Christians in their total population.

**Barbados:**   30% of the women (age 20-45) in a UN national study in 1990, whether previously partnered with someone or not, were victims of domestic abuse during some period of their life. Since the findings represent a population that included people who had not been in a relationship, the rate of domestic violence may have been higher.

**Dominican Republic:** 11% of the women (age 15-49) in a UN national study in 2002, who are or have been married, were victims of domestic abuse within the previous 12 month period. 22% of the women had been subject to domestic violence during some period of their life.

**Ecuador:** From a United Nations (UN) study, 12% of the women (age 15-49) were victims of domestic abuse within the previous 12 month period.

**Great Britain and Ireland:** A study of North London in 1993 found that 12% of women (age > 16) in a UN national study in 1997, who had or had not been in relationships, were victims of domestic abuse within the previous 12 month period. 30% of the women had been subject to domestic violence during some period of their life. In a national study in 2001, 3% of women (age 16-59), who had or had not been in relationships, were victims of domestic violence within the past 12 months. 19% had been subject to domestic abuse since age 16.

Because the results include women who had not been in relationships, the incidence of domestic abuse may have been higher than the reported statistics. A governmental Forced Marriage Unit provides services for 300 cases of forced marriage a year. The government finds that the cost of domestic violence is about £440 per person for a total of 23 billion pounds sterling (£) per year, including the costs of health care, housing, justice, legal, social services and lost output, and suffering.

**Guatemala:** 8% of the women (age 15-49) in a UN national study in 2002, who recently had a partner, were victims of domestic abuse within the previous 12 month period. Studies of women who had been murdered in Guatemala showed a high incidence of domestic violence, honor killings, or dowry disputes as the cause of death. The victims in were also often victims of sexual attacks at the time of their murder.

**Mexico:** From a 1996 UN study on violence against women, 27% of the women (age > 15) in Guadalajara study and 17% of the women (age > 15) in Monterrey, who are or have been married, were victims of domestic violence during some period of their life. 9% of the women (age > 15) in a UN national study in 2003, currently married or partnered, were victims of domestic abuse within the previous 12 month period.

Studies of women who had been murdered in Mexico showed a high incidence of domestic violence, honor killings, or dowry disputes as the cause of death. The victims in were also often victims of sexual attacks at the time of their murder.

There had been a high incidence of abduction, rape and murder of hundreds of women over 10 year period in the Ciudad Juárez, Mexico area that were treated with impunity, treating these cases as "common acts of violence belonging to the private sphere."

The UN Committee found that not investigating nor prosecuting these cases, the "most brutal manifestation [was] extreme violence against women."

**Moldova:** 8% of the women (age 15-44) in a UN national study in 1997, who are or have been married, were victims of domestic abuse within the previous 12 month period. 15% of the women had been subject to domestic violence during some period of their life.

**Papua New Guinea:** 67% of the women (age 15-49) in a UN national, village and rural study in 2002, who are or have been married, were victims of domestic abuse during some period of their life.

**Paraguay:** 10% of the women (age 15-49) in a UN national study in 1995-6, who are or have been married, were victims of domestic abuse during some period of their life. 7% of the women (age 15-44) in a UN national study in 2004, who are or have been married, were victims of domestic abuse within the previous 12 month period; 19% of the women had been subject to domestic violence during some period of their life.

**Peru:** Statistics from three United Nations studies show that 2-25% of married or partnered women (15-49) were victims of domestic abuse within the previous 12 month period. 42-62% of the women had been subject to domestic violence during some period of their life. The studies were performed nationally (2000) with the lowest rate of domestic violence, Lima (2001) and Cusco (2001) with the highest rate of domestic violence.

**Philippines:** 10% of pregnant women (age 15-49) who participated in a UN national study in 1993 were subject to domestic violence during some period of their life. In 1998 in Cagayan de Oro City and Bukidnon, 26% of currently married or partnered women (age 15-49) were subject to domestic violence during some period of their life. 6% of the pregnant women (age 15-49) who participated in a UN national study in 2004 were victims of domestic abuse within the previous 12 month period. 21% of the women had been subject to domestic violence during some period of their life.

**Puerto Rico:** 13% of the women (age 15-49), who participated in a UN national study in 1995-6, who are or have been married, were victims of domestic abuse during some period of their life.

**Romania:** 10% of the women (age 15-44) who participated in a UN national study in 1999, who are or have been married, were victims of domestic abuse within the previous 12 month period. 29% of the women had been subject to domestic violence during some period of their life.

**Samoa:** From a UN national study in 2000, 18% of the women (age 15-49) studied, who are or have been married, were victims of domestic abuse within the previous 12 month period. 41% of the women had been subject to domestic violence during some period of their life.

**Zambia:** 19% of the women (age 15-49) who participated in a UN national study in 2001-2, who are or have been married, were victims of domestic abuse within the previous 12 month period. 47% of the women had been subject to domestic violence during some period of their life.

### National *Domestic violence*

**One in four women (25%) has experienced domestic violence in her lifetime.** (The Centers for Disease Control and Prevention) Estimates range from 960,000 incidents of violence against a current or former spouse, boyfriend, or girlfriend to 3 million women who are physically abused by their husband or boyfriend per year (U.S. Department of Justice, Violence by Intimates).

Women accounted for 85% of the victims of intimate partner violence, men for approximately 15%. (Bureau of Justice Statistics Crime Data Brief, Intimate Partner Violence 1993- 2003).

**Between 600,000 and 6 million women are victims of domestic violence each year, and between 100,000 and 6 million men, depending on the type of survey used to obtain the data.** Intimate partner violence. (National Institute of Justice).

Women ages 20-24 are at the greatest risk of nonfatal intimate partner violence.(Bureau of Justice Statistics, Intimate Partner Violence in the U.S. 1993-2006.)

Between 1993 and 2004, intimate partner violence on average made up 22% of nonfatal intimate partner victimizations against women. The same year, intimate partners committed 3% of all violent crime against men. (Bureau of Justice Statistics, Intimate Partner Violence in the U.S.).

Women of all races are about equally vulnerable to violence by an intimate partner.(Bureau of Justice Statistics, Violence Against Women).

Intimate partner violence affects people regardless of income. However, people with lower annual income (below $25K) are at a 3-times higher risk of intimate partner violence than people with higher annual income (over $50K). (Bureau of Justice Statistics, Intimate Partner Violence in the U.S. 1993- 2006.)

Nearly 2.2 million people called a domestic violence crisis or hot line in 2004 to escape crisis situations, seek advice, or assist some-one they thought might be victims. (National Network to End Domestic Violence).

**Nearly three out of four (74%) of Americans personally know someone who is or has been a victim of domestic violence.** 30% of Americans say they know a woman who has been physically abused by her husband or boyfriend in the past year. (Allstate Foundation National Poll on Domestic Violence, 2006.)

### Domestic Violence Homicides

**On average, more than three women and one man are murdered by their intimate partners in this country every day.** In

2000, 1,247 women were killed by an intimate partner. The same year, 440 men were killed by an intimate partner. Intimate partner homicides accounted for 30% of the murders of women and 5% percent of the murders of men. (Bureau of Justice Statistics Crime Data Brief, Intimate Partner Violence, 1993- 2003. Bureau of Justice Statistics, Intimate Partner Violence)

Most intimate partner homicides occur between spouses, though boyfriends/girlfriends have committed about the same number of homicides in recent years. (Bureau of Justice Statistics, Intimate Partner Violence in the U.S.)

## Health Costs

**The health-related costs of intimate partner violence exceed $5.8 billion each year. Of that amount, nearly $4.1 billion are for direct medical and mental health care services, and nearly $1.8 billion are for the indirect costs of lost productivity or wages.** (Centers for Disease Control and Prevention, Costs of Intimate Partner Violence Against Women in the United States, April 2003.)

About half of all female victims of intimate violence report an injury of some type, and about 20 percent of them seek medical assistance. (National Crime Victimization Survey).

Thirty-seven percent of women who sought treatment in emergency rooms for violence-related injuries in 1994 were injured by a current or former spouse, boyfriend or girlfriend. (U.S. Department of Justice, Violence Related Injuries Treated in Hospital Emergency Departments, 1997).

## Dating violence

Approximately one in five female high school students reports being physically and/or sexually abused by a dating partner. Journal of the American Medical Association, 2001).

Forty percent of girls age 14 to 17 report knowing someone their age who has been hit or beaten by a boyfriend. One in five teens in a serious relationship reports having been hit, slapped, or pushed by a partner. 14% of teens report their boyfriend or girl-friend threatened to harm them or themselves to avoid a break-up. Many studies indicate that as a dating relationship becomes more serious, the potential for and nature of violent behavior also escalates. (Information provided by Oregon Law Center.)

Date rape accounts for almost 70% of sexual assaults reported by adolescent and college age women; 38% of those women are between 14 and 17 years old. (Information provided by Oregon Law Center.)

## Domestic violence and children

### 10 Facts About How Domestic Violence Impacts Kids.

1.  63% of all boys, age 11-20, who commit murder kill the man who was abusing their mother.

2.  75% of boys who are present when their mothers are beaten were later identified as having demonstrable behavior problems.

3.  Children from homes characterized by domestic violence are five to seven times more likely to experience significant psycho-logical problems relative to children in the general population.

4. Domestic violence exposed children are four times more likely to visit the school nurse.

5. More than half of school age children in domestic violence shelters show clinical levels of anxiety or post-traumatic stress disorder.

6. Researchers have linked exposure to chronic abuse and violence with lower IQ scores, poorer language skills, decrements in visual-motor integration skills and problems with attention and memory.

7. Cognitive problems associated with exposure to violence and abuse comprises one of the most direct threats to the developmental task of school adaptation and academic achievement.

8. Witnessing violence as a child is associated with adult reports of depression, trauma-related symptoms and low self-esteem among women and trauma-related symptoms among men.

9. Children in homes where domestic violence occurs are physically abused or seriously neglected at a rate 1500% higher than the national average in the general population.

10. 3.3 million children witness domestic violence each year in the US.

In a national survey of American families, 50% of the men who frequently assaulted their wives also frequently abused their children. (Physical Violence in American Families).

On average between 1993 and 2004, children under age 12 were residents of households experiencing intimate partner violence in 43% of incidents involving female victims and 25% of incidents involving male victims. (Bureau of Justice Statistics, Intimate Partner Violence in the U.S. 1993- 2006.)

**Studies suggest that between 3.3 - 10 million children witness some form of domestic violence annually.** Children as witnesses to marital violence: A risk factor for lifelong problems. (Columbus OH: Ross Laboratories.)

### Domestic violence and male victims

Due to cultural norms that require men to present a strong façade and that minimize female-perpetrated abuse, men are less likely to verbalize fear of any kind. Violence.

### Rape / sexual assault

Three in four women (76%) who reported they had been raped and/or physically assaulted since age 18 said that an intimate partner (current or former husband, cohabiting partner, or date) committed the assault (National Violence Against Women Survey, November 1998).

One in five (21%) women reported she had been raped or physically or sexually assaulted in her lifetime (1998 Survey of Women's Health, 1999).

### Stalking

Annually in the United States, 503,485 women are stalked by an intimate partner (National Institute of Justice, 2000).

One in 12 women and one in 45 men will be stalked in their lifetime, for an average duration of almost two years ("Stalking in America," (U.S. Department of Justice, 1998).

Seventy-eight percent of stalking victims are women. Women are significantly more likely than men (60 percent and 30 percent, respectively) to be stalked by intimate partners. (Center for Policy Research, Stalking in America, July 1997).

Eighty percent of women who are stalked by former husbands are physically assaulted by that partner and 30 percent are sexually assaulted by that partner.( Stalking in America, July 1997).

On average, only 70% of nonfatal partner violence is reported to law enforcement. Of those not reporting, 41% of male and 27% of female victims (34% average) stated victimization being a private/personal matter as reason for not reporting, 15% of women feared reprisal, 12% of all victims wished to protect the offender, and 6% of all victims believed police would do nothing. (Bureau of Justice Statistics, Intimate Partner Violence in the U.S. 1993- 2006.)

The above statistics may shock and amaze some, but all of us at least know someone who has been or still is a victim of Domestic Violence. The roots of this epidemic runs deep in the psyche of both Christian and non-Christians throughout the world; but nevertheless Jesus Christ shed His precious Blood so that we would be Healed and Delivered from ALL physical and emotional bondages, strongholds, curses and the like.

It was never God's intention that marriage---holy matrimony--- be made unholy by the demonic powers---who us human abusers; and thus make that which is good an unhealthy and dangerous union; neither did God intend that other human relationships develop into domestic combat, whereas one or both partners are physically or sexually assaulted or humiliated.

"To death do us part" doesn't mean that we should accept death rather than part company; any type of abusive behavior from a spouse, romantic or personal relationship such as dating, is unacceptable. In the case of the married, separation and even divorce should be considered as a legal and scriptural solution. Sadly, many have taken the mater to its extreme, and committed suicide, murder, manslaughter or even justifiable homicide, to get out of this type of relationship.

It is also the deviance of the enemy to control the man in a relationship by manipulating the Criminal Justice System. This is done by female partners who use the law to control the behavior of her husband or boyfriend. This includes filing false police reports of abuse or threatening to do so, alleging violence or threats when nothing of the kind has happened.

The goal is to punish a partner who wants to think and act independently, or who wants to leave or has left the relationship; often jealousy of another woman---real or imagined evidence---leads to such demonic, vindictive behavior. It is a spirit of Jezebel---control and manipulation that leads a woman to "tap" into the resources of the police department to control or punish a mate.

Still many victims of Domestic Violence are afraid to come forth---often intimidated by the abuser or his/her family---and even the local pastor may tell him/her to drop the charge against her spouse, because it's the "Christian" thing to do. And after the initial threat is over, he/she fails to follow through in the Court; and thus the abuser is set free to come home and do it again, and thus the cycle of abuse continues, and even the children suffer.

The End

www.ingramcontent.com/pod-product-compliance
Lightning Source LLC
Chambersburg PA
CBHW071830020426
42331CB00007B/1681